The Best of Frances Browne

Poems, Stories and Essays
by the Blind Genius
of Stranorlar
Introduced and Arranged by Raymond Blair

ISBN: 978-0-9571802-0-8

Published by:
Rathmore Books,
18 Rathmore road,
Limavady
BT49 0DF

Copyright:
©Raymond Blair, 2012

Printed by:
Browne printers, Letterkenny, Co. Donegal
tel. +353 (0)74 9121387

DEDICATION

In memory of my father, the late Joseph Blair of Cavan Upper, Killygordon, County Donegal, who passed on to me a great love for both history and poetry.

Stranorlar Historical Park, showing the opening line from Songs of our Land.

THE BEST OF FRANCES BROWNE (1816-1879)

'The bards may go down to the place of their slumbers,
    The lyre of the charmer be hushed in the grave,
    But far in the future the power of their numbers
    Shall kindle the hearts of our faithful and brave,
    It will waken an echo in souls deep and lonely,
Like the voices of reeds by the summer breeze fanned;
    It will call up a spirit for freedom, when only
    Her breathings are heard in the songs of our land.'

From: *Songs of our Land* by Frances Browne, 1841

Contents

Acknowledgments ... 9
List of Illustrations ... 11

Introduction ... 13

Section I - Poems
To The Great Western, Outward Bound ... 21
The Land of The Slave ... 23
The Poet's Wealth ... 25
Oh The Pleasant Days of Old ... 28
Going Home ... 29
Losses ... 32
Is It Come? ... 34
The Winters ... 36
The Wild-Swan ... 38
The Children's Day ... 41

Section II – Short Stories
The Lost New-Year's Gift ... 42
Benoni's Mourning ... 57
Panhoe Pan and Her Seven Suitors ... 64
The Wreckers of Fannet ... 73
Nelly MacAdam ... 89
Disappointment Hall ... 101
The Forgotten Chest ... 110

Section III – Essays
Half-Way People ... 127
A Chapter on Odd People ... 133
The Philosophy of Would Be ... 140
Letters ... 149

The Little People Of Our Great Towns 161

Appendix I
Frances Browne, Timeline 165

Appendix II
Original Contributions to Newspapers etc. 166

Appendix III
Further Reading 169

Appendix IV
Tribute Poem 171

Acknowledgements

The extensive research which made this book possible has been carried out with the assistance of the staff from many libraries. First and foremost, the National Library of Scotland is to be thanked for alerting me to the stories and essays by Frances Browne to be found in *Chambers's Edinburgh Journal,* and for helping me to obtain copies of these. The crucial help of Miss Ruth Boreham, historical researcher, in identifying the contributions that Frances Browne made to that Journal, is gladly acknowledged. She also got copies of other items for me that would have been very awkward to obtain by any other means.

The other repositories that provided me with vital assistance were the British Library in London, the National Library of Ireland, Cambridge University Library (which helped me to get a copy of *The Forgotten Chest*), the Belfast Central Library (especially the Newspaper section of that institution) and the Derry City Library. The few days spent in the British Library were very fruitful as I was able to consult the records of the Royal Literary Fund (of which Frances became a beneficiary in the 1860's) which revealed the scale of her contributions to several hitherto undiscovered magazines.

Warmest thanks are due to Mr Paddy Bonar, author of the only modern biography of the poetess, for being the one who first stimulated my interest in the life of Frances Browne. I am also grateful to Celine McGlynn, Pat Holland, and the staff of the *Finn Valley Voice* for featuring so many of my discoveries in the columns of the newspaper. I was also greatly aided in my research by the 'Google Books' search engine, which brought to light quite a few of Browne's compositions that I might not otherwise have come across. For instance, the story, *Panhoe Pan and her Seven Suitors* was first identified via this online search facility.

The photograph on the front cover, the only known likeness of Frances Browne, was initially supplied by Mrs Selwyn Glynn of Brisbane, a relative of the authoress. Thanks also to my friend, Allister Doey, for the fine photos of the Stranorlar Historical Park and of the boulder in

Drumboe Woods. Finally, I would like to acknowledge the encouragement given by my wife Carole, and by my daughters, Eileanoir, Labhaoise, Rosaleen and Iona, in the course of the many hours that I have spent on this project,

Raymond Blair, Limavady, January 2012.

List of Illustrations

Front Cover
Only known photograph of the blind poetess.

Page 4
Stranorlar Historical Park, showing the first line from *Songs of our Land*.

Page 15
Old photograph of Stranorlar, County Donegal, the town where Frances Browne was born in 1816.

Page 16
The Blind Girl at Home – from *Clever Girls of our Time* by Joseph Johnson (1862).

Page 20
Boulder in Drumboe Woods near Stranorlar inscribed with some lines from *A Parting Voice*, composed in 1847.

Page 22
The Great Western, the revolutionary steamship which inspired Browne's poem, *To The Great Western, Outward Bound*.

Page 29
The Music to *Going Home*, one of several poems by Browne that were set to music.

Page 40
Edinburgh – Frances Browne lived in Edinburgh from 1847 until 1852.

Page 50
Dressmaker's establishment in London – it portrays the hard labour of the young women who worked long hours for little pay.

Page 88
The Neighbours of Kilmaclone – another story by Browne which was set in Ireland.

Page 95
The Evening Prayer – taken from *Pictures and Songs of Home, 2nd edition* (1861).

Page 108
Butler Ward Acts the Gallant – taken from the *Welcome Guest* (1860-61).

Page 124
The Discovery of the Gold Coins – from *The Forgotten Chest* (1893).

Page 132
Title page of *Chambers's Edinburgh Journal* (1845).

Page 155
Richmond-upon-Thames – Frances Browne lived there between 1866 and 1879.

Page 163
Gathering Wild Flowers, taken from *Pictures and Songs of Home* (1861).

Introduction

> *'Behold, how still the world rewards*
> *Her brightest, as of yore;*
> *For then she gave a nameless grave –*
> *And now she gives no more!'*

Frances Browne of Stranorlar, County Donegal, lies buried in an unmarked grave somewhere in the overgrown public cemetery in Richmond-upon-Thames. Therefore, the lines cited above from her poem, *The Ancient Tombs*, are very applicable to her own experience. Although she attained a fair degree of fame as a writer during the Victorian era, she was very quickly forgotten about after her death. Most people today in Britain and her native Ireland know nothing at all about her. It is out of a firm conviction that she deserves to be better remembered that this anthology has been put together.

The anthology aims to collect in one place a selection of the poems, short stories and essays of the author who was widely known in her lifetime as the 'Blind Poetess of Ulster'. A timeline of the main events of her life is contained in Appendix I, and a fuller account of her career can be found in the works that are recommended for further reading (Appendix III). Suffice it to say at this stage that, despite being struck blind by smallpox in the year 1817, at the early age of 18 months, she managed, through determined effort, to educate herself. This was no easy task given her modest social background: she was one of 12 children of the Stranorlar postmaster, Samuel Browne. Eventually, in 1840, she boldly embarked on a literary career that ultimately took her from her home village of Stranorlar to the great literary centres of Edinburgh and London. By the time of her death in 1879, at the age of 63, she had produced a wide range of works, many of which were of the highest quality.

This book doesn't deal with some of her better known works as these can be easily accessed via modern reprints or read online by means of 'Google Books.' Therefore, you will not find here anything from *Granny's Wonderful Chair*, although it is generally regarded as her best piece of writing – it has been reprinted many times since its first appearance in 1856, and is still readily available. Generations of children have been held spellbound by its highly imaginative fantasy tales. Not included either are her three published anthologies of poetry, *The Star of Atteghei, Lyrics and Miscellaneous Poems,* and *Pictures and Songs of Home.* Two of these are available in modern reprints. No attention either is given to her three major novels, *My share of the World, The Castleford Case,* and *The Hidden Sin.* Such is the scale of these novels a completely separate volume would be needed to deal with them thoroughly. Indeed, given her industriousness, there is much more that had to be omitted. What will be found here are the best of her uncollected poems, short stories and essays.

Considerable research has been undertaken in order to uncover pieces that were scattered far and wide in the many newspapers, journals and periodicals to which the blind poetess contributed. There were many such pieces but only those considered either of higher quality, or of most interest, have been selected – sufficient to whet the reader's appetite. But, it is also hoped that the sample will help to restore the reputation of this quite brilliant woman who has, until recently, been undeservedly forgotten. A full list of the newspapers, journals and magazines to which Frances is known to have made original contributions (as distinct from having her works copied and reprinted which happened a lot) is given in Appendix II as an aid to further research. It has to be acknowledged, however, in the light of how prolific she was as a writer, that this is probably far from being a complete list. Nevertheless, it will give the reader some idea of how widely she cast her literary net. It will also be evident that many of the magazines were aimed at a female readership. For example, although we have not chosen to include any in this anthology, it can be seen that Frances made numerous contributions in the 1850's to *The Ladies' Companion,* one of the most fashionable magazines for well-to-do ladies of that era. One such contribution, of 1853, which may be accessed on the Web by means of the 'Google Books' search engine, is called *Mrs Sloper's Swan*; it is a very amusing story about how a snobbish London lady is brought down more that a peg or two!

Happily, there is much renewed interest in her career in the locality of Stranorlar. Patrick Bonar's book on her life and works (see further reading) was an important step forward and the local newspaper, the *Finn Valley Voice*, has even sponsored a poetry competition in her honour. There is also some evidence of a growing academic interest in her literary output. It is particularly gratifying to see that she has been included in the recent multi-volume magisterial Dictionary of Irish Biography. Nevertheless, there is still much more to be found out about her literary career and plenty of scope for a full scale, scholarly biography.

In the first section, ten poems by Frances Browne are to be found. It is fitting that we begin with her poetry as this was always her greatest source of enjoyment and fulfilment. In the autobiographical preface to *The Star of Atteghei*, she writes, 'From my earliest years, I had a great and strange love of poetry' and she refers to having had 'an irresistible inclination to poetry.' Her most famous poem, *Songs of our Land* is too widely available to be fully included here; however, a short excerpt, in which Frances expresses her belief in the enduring power of poetry, is cited near the beginning of this book. A biographical sketch in *Chambers's Journal* of 1861 perceptively stated that her poems were her 'best biography.' Her poems were said to reveal 'her energy of mind, her resolution of character, her scorn of mean and soulless men, her love of the brave, the wise and the good.'

This anthology includes *To the Great Western, Outward Bound* which was the first piece of writing by the poetess to appear in print; it appeared in *The Londonderry Standard* in June of 1840. As was often the case, this poem was inspired by a major news story of the time – the speedy voyages from Britain to America by a steamship designed by Isambard Kingdom Brunel. The tenth poem in this anthology, *The Chil-*

Old photo of Stranorlar, the town where Frances was born in 1816.

dren's Day, was the last piece she ever wrote, having been penned just a few days before her death. It is not, perhaps, her most impressive composition, but it does reveal her sympathy for the children of the poor as well as her love for the beauty of the countryside. She portrays the little children returning from their trip to the countryside to 'the crowded homes and the lowly beds/Where the poor and the toiling lay their heads.'

The ten poems included highlight some of the key themes found in her writing – her opposition to slavery, her religious faith, her sympathy

The Blind Girl at Home, taken from Clever Girls of our Time *by Joseph Johnson (1862).*

for the poor and oppressed, her disillusionment with the greed and materialism of the industrial age, the exile's longing for home, and her belief in the value of poetry as a source of enrichment for mind and spirit. For example, in *The Poet's Wealth,* Frances acknowledged that the 'riches of our heritage' did not consist in worldly wealth but 'in thought, and song, and summer skies/Its changeless wealth lies yet secure.' Indeed, in *The Wild-Swan,* written ten years later, she bemoaned the lack of interest which a materialistic culture had in the finer things such as poetry.

Some pieces, such as *The Winters,* are dominated by the note of melancholy that was so characteristic of her poetry. Consider, for instance, this extract from the poem – 'Alas! dear friends, the winter is within us/ Hard is the ice that grows about the heart;' Thus, her fellow-Donegal writer, Seumas MacManus, once described her as 'one who so sweetly sang the sad songs of her land.' On the other hand, *Oh! The Pleasant Days of Old,* strikes the humorous note that can be found more often in her essays and short stories. Included also, is the poem, *Is it Come?* This sophisticated composition so impressed the 3rd Marquis of Lansdowne that, shortly after its appearance in 1855, and on hearing that the poetess was struggling financially, he sent her a substantial gift of £100. Readers will come across the poem, *Losses,* which has been classified as a masterpiece of religious verse, and which is easily her most frequently reprinted poem. In common with many of her poems, it was first published in *The Athenaeum,* the prestigious London periodical that did so much to advance Browne's literary reputation. The other poem in this anthology likewise taken from the pages of *The Athenaeum* is called *Going Home* and is very religious in outlook; it also had the distinction of being set to music! Indeed, a detailed analysis of her religious thought and its development over the course of her life would make for a very interesting book.

In the second section, seven short stories, from the hundreds that Frances penned, have been selected for your enjoyment. Paul Marchbanks (see further reading), in a recent scholarly appraisal of her writing, rightly refers to her 'compelling storytelling skills.' Three of the seven chosen stories are taken from *Chambers's Edinburgh Journal,* a very popular periodical in Victorian Britain. In fact, research conducted in the Chambers's Archive in the National Library of Scotland, revealed that she wrote over 100 items for the journal between 1845 and 1870, mostly short stories, but also some essays and a few poems. Notes of romance, humour and tragedy, so typical of her prose, are evident in the three stories selected. In particular, *The Lost New-Year's Gift,* (the first prose piece that she had published) is a very moving story of the struggles and tragic death of a poor seamstress in London.

There is an interesting Irish background to the tale, *Nelly Macadam,* another not uncommon feature in the stories of Frances Browne. As with *The Lost New-Year's Gift,* this story has a young impoverished heroine at its centre but on this occasion there is a happy and even a romantic ending to the adventure. *Benoni's Mourning* displays a fine perception of the human capacity for self-delusion, and seems to have been modelled on the style of her famous contemporary, Charles Dickens. His brilliant, *A Christmas Carol,* had only appeared a few years previously and there are some close parallels between it and the tale about Benoni.

Although living in London at the right time, no evidence exists that Frances ever crossed paths with Dickens but some of her writing is certainly influenced by his style. It is a testimony to her high profile that, when in 1852 *The Lady's Newspaper* drew up a list of 'Women of the Time,' the name of Frances Browne is found listed alongside such notables as Mrs S.C. Hall, Mrs Barrett Browning and the 'authoress of Jane Eyre.' In fact, it is worth quoting from the recollections of a fellow-writer, Mrs Newton Crosland (*Landmarks of a Literary Life,*) who encountered Frances Browne shortly after her arrival in London in the early 1850's:-

'The present generation seems to know nothing of Frances Brown, the blind poetess; but about the middle of the century her name was well before the world, and a few years later, her merits were sufficiently recognised for her to receive a government pension... Her memory was most retentive, and her mind singularly receptive, for she seemed fairly well acquainted with the topics of the day and its current publications, and better still, with many sterling works which are the glories of English literature.'

Four other stories, drawn from some of the many other organs for which she wrote, have been selected. The very amusing tale, *Panhoe Pan and her Seven Suitors,* is set in China and serves to illustrate Browne's fascination with exotic locations. On the other hand, *Disappointment Hall,* is set in Ireland and is a powerful critique of human greed and vanity. The other Irish-based tale, *The Wreckers of Fannet,* is one of 12 Legends of Ulster which appeared in *Tait's Edinburgh Magazine* between 1849 and 1851, and it alerts us to her familiarity with the lore of the countryside. Indeed, *The Wreckers of Fannet* should be of special interest to Donegal folk as it is set in the north of the county. It is a highly embellished account of a real historical event – the sinking of the *Saldanha* frigate off the Donegal coast in 1811. The last story included, *The Forgotten Chest,* has only been discovered very recently and was one of many religious pieces that Frances wrote for the Religious Tract Society. The version discovered is of a date long after her death but it is likely that it originally appeared as one of her many contributions to the periodicals of the Religious Tract Society. Even this story has a strong historical element to it, reflecting the author's fascination with history. In her early years, she had been chiefly interested in works of fiction but later became more attached to what she called 'the far more wonderful romance of history.'

The third section of this anthology focuses on five of her essays. Her skills as an essayist have generally been overlooked. As these selections demonstrate, she was in fact a very accomplished practitioner of this lost art – the great erudition and the exquisite humour of these essays should be evident. As she was a keen observer of the foibles and follies of mankind, it is no surprise to come across her rather scathing essay on *Half-Way People*. Her sense of humour is to the fore in *A Chapter on Odd People*. Special attention should be given to the short piece, *The Little People of our Great Towns,* in that it displays her deep concern for the children of the urban poor. The somewhat longer essay, *The Philosophy of Would Be,* provides a good example of her amazingly wide store of knowledge and her fine mastery of the English language. Given that she was the daughter of a postmaster, it is not surprising to find an essay entitled *Letters* which makes for fascinating reading. Some of these essays draw on experiences from her early days in Donegal for illustrative material; for example, in *The Little People of our Great Towns*, there are lyrical descriptions of the Donegal countryside which are contrasted with the greyness of the urban environment of the great towns.

This anthology draws to a close (Appendix IV) with a tribute poem written in honour of the poetess. It captures well in verse what we have been attempting to express in prose about the remarkable achievements of Frances Browne. Alicia Jane Sparrow, expressing her wonder at the beauty of Browne's writing, exclaimed, 'Oh, what can bring these glorious things before thy darken'd eye.' Given not only her severe disability, but also gender disadvantage, modest social background and geographical isolation, one can only be amazed at all that she achieved. Therefore, it is hoped that this anthology will help to convince a modern readership that the 'Blind Poetess of Ulster' fully deserves to be called the 'Blind Genius of Stranorlar.'

Boulder in Drumboe Woods, near Stranorlar, inscribed with some words from A Parting Voice which Frances wrote just before leaving Stranorlar for Edinburgh in 1847. The inscription is faded but ends with the poignant words, 'yet fare-thee-well, my land!'

Section I - Poems

1. To the Great Western, Outward Bound

Go, matchless as the winged light!
Upon thy ocean way,
Thou scorner of the winds in flight,
More swift and sure than they!
To the far realm of forests bear
Our old world's greeting free,
With power to bring the distant near,
Thou conqueror of the sea!

For many a bark before the gale
Hath sought thy sunset track,
But none the watcher's eye may hail
So soon, so surely, back;
And welcome, even as springs that shine
Beneath the desert star,
Thou comest to the hearts that pine
For tidings from afar.

Go, glorious messenger unspent
The hope of parted climes,
Thou seemest as an earnest sent,
Of the world's better times;
When science, mighty on the earth,
Shall change all dross to gold,
And leave no part for waste or dearth,
As sung the muse of old.

God keep thy lone way o'er the wave
At morn or midnight hour,
From arrows of the lightning safe,
And from the tempest's power;
For records of their love and faith,
Which true hearts trust to thee,
A blessing be around thy path,
Swift traveller of the sea!

Source: *Londonderry Standard*, 17th *June 1840*

The Great Western steamship which inspired Browne's poem To the Great Western, Outward Bound.

2. The Land of the Slave

The boy made his rest, where, for ages waved on
One tree of a forest, whose thousands were gone;
But the soft Summer airs through its foliage still played,
And the wild birds rejoiced in the depth of its shade.
Oh! broad was the river, and lovely the scene,
That spread where the wilds of that forest had been,
The noon lay, in splendour, on field and on wave,
But the boy knew it shone on the Land of the Slave.

And well might he cast his young limbs on the soil;
Their grace was for fetters, their strength was for toil;
For the current that blent with his life-stream was one,
That burst, in far time, by the fount of the sun.
Oh! dark was the midnight that shadowed it course,
But his eye was still lit by the fire of that source;
For the changeless old charter, that liberty gave,
Hath a record still left in the Land of the Slave.

But, where might that weary eye rest, when it sought
Some spot where the brand of his memory was not?
He turned from the fields, with their Summer wealth filled,
For he knew in what terror their furrows were tilled;
He looked on the river, and thought of the day
Its waters had wafted his kindred away,
And the tears of the young that had blent with its wave;
But, alas! for bright youth in the Land of the Slave.

He saw the far sky, like an ocean of blue
And thought of the mother his infancy knew -
Of the love that through toil and through bondage she bore,
And the night-coming step that might seek him no more.
Oh! faint was the faith of his future, and dim
The hope that soul-masters had granted to him;
But they said that the grass had grown green on her grave,
And he wished her not back to the Land of the Slave.

Yet, ever the birds, on the branches above,
Sang on in the joy of their freedom and love –
Their freedom, that sceptre or sword never cleft,
Their love, on which tyrants no footprints had left.
And oh! for their lot, where a shadow ne'er crossed
The light of the Summers his childhood had lost,
For their song that burst forth, like a stream from its cave,
And their wings that could waft from the Land of the Slave.

Young lover of freedom, that prayer was not vain,
Though far was the moment that shivered thy chain;
But woe for the heart that can find in the clime
Of its early remembrance but deserts of time!
Our isle hath her sorrows; the page of her years
Is dark with the memory of discord and tears;
But she still owns the heart and the hand that would save,
And we welcome thy steps from the Land of the Slave.

Source: *The Northern Whig, 10th January 1846.*

Note: This poem was written on the occasion of the visit of the escaped slave, Frederick Douglass, to Ireland in 1846 – hence the greeting that Frances bestowed upon his "steps from the Land of the Slave."

3. The Poet's Wealth

*We are not poor old friend, though years
Of toil have brought us only bread,
And such small shelter as appears
Most like a pilgrim's shed.
Though this world's glory and its gold
Have passed us by as wights obscure
Our liberty was never sold
For them or theirs, we are not poor.*

*Wealth cannot buy nor custom bound
The thoughts that give us regal days,
Through many burdens and the round
Of petty wants and worldly ways.
The glimpse of truth that makes us free
To know the right from power and gain,-
However, crowds or creeds may see,
We have not trimmed the lamp in vain.*

*Its light hath scattered many a dream
That hid the poverty of life,-
And showed how near the clay-mark came
Its baseless lore, its bootless strife.
We had a hope of better things,
Perchance it might not long endure
The knowledge that each dark year brings,-
Yet for its sake we are not poor.*

*Time has not mocked us with the smile
And hush for which his vassals wait;
But we learned in spite of toil
And we have climbed in spite of fate.
Woe worth the wanderings and the wars
Wherein our souls so grey have grown,
And ill befall the luckless stars
That made us strangers to our own.*

And yet we found us friends among
The earth's great thoughts and names – and grew
As of that race by page and song
Even leaders to the nation, too.
Their homes that rest in fortune's lights,
Their crowds of graves and burdens sure,
Are debtors to our sleepless nights,
Cheer up, old friend, we are not poor.
Alas their fruit is small beside,
The early promise of our field!
Yet let the few full ears abide
To tell what might have been its yield.
Had hope some better harvest lent
Than those that made our memory old,
Of faith found false, of hope grown faint,
Of friendship turned unkind and cold.

The waters will not render back
The bread cast on them to our age,-
Well, friend, it was but crumbs and not
The riches of our heritage.
In thought, and songs, and summer skies,
Its changeless wealth lies yet secure,
Though wastes of care and work-days rise
Twixt us and it – we are not poor.

The goddess of the common faith
Whom all invoke and many blame
What though for us her quiver hath
But shafts that never miss their aim,-
We mourn for ills she never brought
We joy in goods she cannot steal.
Yet woe for some whom fortune brought
And made the bondsmen of her wheel.
The voice that spoke was free and clear
The heart had little left to lose,-
And they that kept such kindly cheer

Were but a poet and his Muse.
Perchance he sought no other mate
Perchance his fortunes could allure
None else to share the bard's estate,-
Yet with that friend he was not poor.

Source: *The Athenaeum, 1851*

4. Oh! The Pleasant Days of Old

Oh! the pleasant days of old, which so often people praise –
True, they wanted all the luxuries that grace our modern days;
Bare floors were strewed with rushes – the walls let in the cold;
Oh! how they must have shivered in those pleasant days of old!

Oh! those ancient lords of old, how magnificent they were!
They threw down and imprisoned kings, to thwart them who might dare;
They ruled their serfs right sternly; they took from Jews their gold-
Above both law and equity were those great lords of old!

Oh! the gallant knights of old, for their valour so renowned;
With sword and lance, and armour strong, they scoured the country round;
And whenever aught to tempt them they met by wood or wold,
By right of sword they seized the prize - those gallant knights of old!

Oh! the gentle dames of old, who, quite free from fear or pain,
Could gaze on joust and tournament and see their champions slain;
They lived on good beefsteaks and ale, which made them strong and bold;
Oh! more like men than women were those gentle dames of old!

Oh! those mighty towers of old, with their turrets, moat and keep,
Their battlements and bastions, their dungeons dark and deep,
Full many a baron held his court within his castle hold,
And many a captive languished there in those strong towers of old!

Oh! the troubadours of old, with their gentle minstrelsie,
Of hope and joy, or deep despair, whiche'er their lot might be –
For years they served their lady love, e'er their passion told –
Oh! wondrous patience must have had those troubadours of old!

Oh! those blessed times of old, with their chivalry and state;
I love to read their chronicles, which such brave deeds relate –
I love to sing their ancient rhymes, to hear their legends told –
But, heaven be thanked, I live not in those blessed times of old!

Source: *Bentley's Miscellany*, 1851.

5. Going Home

We said that the days were evil,
We felt that they might be few,
For low was our fortune's level,
And heavy the winters grew;
But one who had no possession
Looked up to the azure dome,
And said in his simple fashion,
Dear friends, we are going home!

This world is the same dull market,
That wearied its earliest sage:
The times to the wise are dark yet,
But so hath been many an age.
And rich grow the toiling nations,
And red grow the battle spears,
And dreary with desolations
Roll onward the laden years.

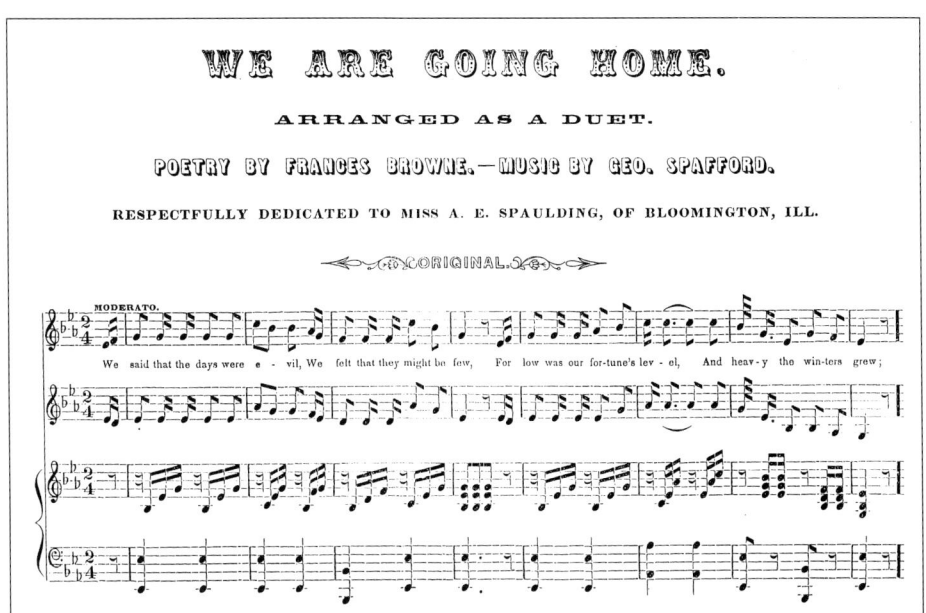

The music to Going Home, one of several of Browne's poems to be set to music.

*What need of the changeless story
Which time hath so often told,
The spectre that follows glory,
The canker that comes with gold, -
That wisdom and strength and honour
Must fade like the far sea foam,
And Death is the only winner, -
But, friends, we are going home!*

*The homes we had hoped to rest in
Were open to sin and strife,
The dreams that our youth was blessed in
Were not for the wear of life;
For care can darken the cottage,
As well as the palace hearth,
And birthrights are sold for pottage,
But never redeemed on earth.*

*The springs have gone by in sorrow,
The summers were grieved away,
And ever we feared to-morrow,
And ever we blamed to-day.
In depths which the searcher sounded,
On hills which the high heart clomb,
Have trouble and toil abounded: -
But, friends, we are going home!*

*Our faith was the bravest builder,
But found not a stone of trust;
Our love was the fairest gilder,
But lavished its wealth on dust.
And time hath the fabric shaken,
And fortune, the clay hath shown,
For much they have changed and shaken,
But nothing that was our own.*

The light that to us made baser
The paths which so many choose,
The gifts there was found no place for,
The riches we could not use;
The heart that when life was wintry
Found summer in strain and tome,
With these to our kin and country: -
Dear, friends, we are going home!

Source: *The Athenaeum, 31st March 1855.*

6. Losses

Upon the white sea-sand
There sat a pilgrim band,
Telling the losses that their lives had known,
While evening waned away
From breezy cliff and bay,
And the strong tides went out with weary moan.

One spake with quivering lip,
Of a fair freighted ship,
With all his household to the deep gone down:
But one had wilder woe
For a fair face, long ago
Lost in the darker depths of a great town.

There were who mourned their youth,
With a most loving ruth,
For its brave hopes and memories ever green;
And one upon the West
Turned an eye that would not rest
For far-off hills whereon its joy had been.

Some talked of vanished gold,
Some of proud honours told,
Some spake of friends that were their trust no more;
And one of a green grave,
Beside a foreign wave,
That made him sit so lonely on the shore.

But when their tales were done,
There spake among them one,
A stranger, seeming from all sorrow free, -
"Sad losses have ye met
But mine is heavier yet,

For a believing heart hath gone from me."
"Alas!" these pilgrims said,
"For the living and the dead,
For fortune's cruelty, for love's sure cross,
For wrecks of land and sea!
But, however it came to thee,
Thine, stranger, is life's last and heaviest loss."

Source: *The Athenaeum, 7TH July 1855.*

7. Is It Come?

Is it come? They said on the banks of the Nile,
Who looked for the world's long-promised day,
And saw but the strife of Egypt's toil
With the desert's sands and the granite grey.
From pyramid, temple, and treasured dead
We vainly ask for her wisdom's plan;
They tell of the slave and tyrant's dread, -
Yet there was hope when that day began.

The Chaldee came with his starry lore,
That built up Babylon's crown and creed;
And bricks were stamped on the Tigris' shore
With signs that our sages scarce can read.
From Ninus' temple and Nimrod's tower
The rule of the old East's empire spread,
Unreasoning faith and unquestioned power –
But still, Is it come? the Watcher said.

The light of the Persian's worshipped flame,
On ancient bondage its splendour threw;
And once on the West a sunrise came,
When Greece to her freedom's trust was true.
With dreams to the utmost ages dear,
With human gods and with godlike men,
No marvel the far-off day seemed near
To eyes that looked through her laurels then.

The Roman conquered and revelled, too,
Till honour and faith and power were gone;
And deeper old Europe's darkness grew
As wave after wave the Goth came on.
The gown was learning, the sword was law,
The people served in the oxen's stead;
But ever some gleam the Watcher saw,
And evermore, Is it come? they said.

Poet and Seer that question caught
Above the din of life's fears and frets;
It marched with letters - it toiled with thought,
Through schools and creeds which the earth forgets;
And statesmen trifle, and priests deceive,
And traders barter our world away;
Yet hearts to that golden promise cleave,
And still, at times, Is it come? they say.

The days of the nations bear no trace
Of all the sunshine so far foretold;
The cannon speaks in the Teacher's place –
The age is weary with work and gold; -
And high hopes wither and memories wane –
On hearths and altars the fires are dead;
But that brave faith hath not lived in vain: -
And this is all that our Watcher said.

Source: *The Athenaeum, 18th August 1855*

8. The Winters

We did not fear them once – the dull grey mornings
No cheerless burden on our spirits laid;
The long night-watches did not bring us warnings
That we were tenants of a house decayed;
The early snows like dreams to us descended;
The frost did fairy-work on pane and bough.
Beauty, and power, and wonder, have not ended –
How is it that we fear the winters now?

Their home-fires fall as bright on hearth and chamber
Their northern starlight shines as coldly clear;
The woods still keep their holly for December;
The world a welcome yet for the new year;
And far away in old-remembered places
The snowdrop rises and the robin sings;
The sun and moon look out with loving faces –
Why have our days forgot these goodly things?

Is it that now the north wind finds us shaken
By tempests fiercer than its bitter blast,
Which fair beliefs, and friendships, too, have taken
Away like summer foliage as they passed,
And made life leafless in its pleasant valleys,
Waning the light of promise from our day,
Till the mists meet even in the inward palace –
A dimness not like theirs to pass away?

It was not thus when dreams of love and laurels
Gave sunshine to the winters of our youth,
Before its hopes had fallen in fortune's quarrels,
Or time had bowed them with his heavy truth –
Ere yet the twilights found us strange and lonely,
With shadows coming when the fire burns low,
To tell of distant graves and losses only –
The past that cannot change and will not go.

Alas! dear friends, the winter is within us,
Hard is the ice that grows about the heart;
For petty cares and vain regrets have won us
From life's true heritage and better part.
Seasons and skies rejoice, yea, worship rather;
But nations toil and tremble even as we,
Hoping for harvests they will never gather,
Fearing the winters which they may not see.

Source: *The Illustrated London News*, 22nd *December 1855.*

9. The Wild-Swan

An arrow sent from the hunter's string,
When the moorland sky was gray,
Had smote the strength of the wild-swan's wing,
On his far and upward way.
Pinion and plume of vigour reft,
Drooped like boughs by the tempest cleft
On some green forest tree,
And never might the wild swan soar
To the purple heights of morning more;
Or westward o'er the hill-tops cleave
His course through the cloudy skies of eve,
And the sunset's golden sea.

The light of the lovely lakes that lie
Among green woods was gone
From all his days, but the years went by,
And the lonely swan lived on,
A captive bound to the dull earth then,
With wingless creatures and weary men
Who could not quit the clay;
He grew like them, as a dweller must.
At home with the dullness and the dust,
Till faded from his memory's hold
The life and liberty of old,
Like a far forgotten day.

Yet ever as from wood and wave
The smile of the summer went,
And his kindred's march passed south, above
The spot where he was pent,
With their wavy lines and their wings of snow,
And their trumpet's notes sent far below
To bid that lingerer rise,
The swan would gaze as the host swept by,

And a wild regret was in his cry,
As if for the nobler part and place
He lost in the freedom of his race –
In the joy of streams and skies.

Falls not the wild-swan's fortune oft
On souls that scorn the ground,
With outspread wings the deadly shaft
Of an earthward fate hath found;
And narrowed down to some dusty scope
The tameless strength and the tireless hope
That for the skies were born;
Till in the lore of that lifeless lot
Their glorious birthright seems forgot,
As dimness deepens and grayness grows,
And year by year with its burden goes
To the night that knows no morn?

Yet over the prison-house at times,
Great thoughts and voices go,
That wake with the mind-world's mighty chimes,
Their buried life below;
And the bowed of bondage lift their view,
To the heaven that lies so far and blue
In its boundless beauty yet,
But never can they that realm regain,
The wing is withered, the cry is vain –
So downward turn they, eye and heart,
And learn, but not with a ready heart,
Of that wild-swan – 'Forget!'

Source: *Chambers's Journal*, 1861

Edinburgh: Frances lived there between 1847 and 1852.

10. The Children's Day

From streets and traffic and schools away
They have been with the summer for a day
In the leafy woods; on the grassy hills;
Where the flowers grow thick by the meadow rills,
On the broad old river's banks of green,
With the breeze and the sunshine they have been.

And now as the western sun wears low,
Weary but joyous home they go
To father and mother, kin and friends,
That look for them as the long day ends,
To the crowded homes and the lowly beds
Where the poor and the toiling lay their heads.

But will not the sleep that finds them there
Bring back the sweets of the woodland air,
And lend to their after hours of dreams
The light that lay on those hills and streams?
For thus when the happy day is gone
Its happier memories linger on.

Bright mornings break on the kindly heart,
That first in the summer gave them part,
And poor men's children in cities pent
Forth to the feast of nature sent,
To learn from the beauty spread abroad
How great, how good were the works of God!

Source: *The Sunday at Home*, 1879

Section II – Short Stories

1. The Lost New-Year's Gift

It was the last day of the year – the last dress of Lady Fitzalbert's costly mourning had just been finished, and the working girls of one of the largest millinery establishments in London were dismissed to seek their distant homes at three o'clock on a December morning. The frost was keen and clear, and the wind, which swept through the now silent and deserted streets, sent a chill to the hearts of that worn-out company, as on they passed by many a noble mansion, and many an ample warehouse. None spoke for they had talked themselves out in the workroom; none looked up, though the London sky was for once without a cloud, and the stars were shining there as they shone when London was a forest. But heart, and brain, and eye had been exhausted by two days of continued labour, and they thought of nothing but hurrying home to sleep. One after another parted from the group with a murmured good night as they reached their respective dwellings till at last none was left but Lucy Lever whose home happened to be the most distant of all.

Lucy was a young and beautiful girl of eighteen, whose bright blue eyes, golden hair, and fair transparent complexion might have graced a prouder station. She was the daughter of a poor country tradesman, who had some years before removed to London with his family, in hopes of bettering their fortunes, but died soon after one of those fatal epidemics which so often visit the poorer habitations of our large towns. The mother had struggled on, through poverty and toil to have her eldest daughter instructed in needlework and to maintain two younger daughters; but a severe attack of rheumatism which at length became chronic, had totally unfitted her for her laborious employment as a washerwoman, and the whole burthen of the family support fell upon Lucy, whose small earnings were barely sufficient to keep them from absolute want.

They had one friend in London, the sister of Lucy's mother, who was married to a small shopkeeper, accounted rich among his class; but, like too many of the rich in every class, possessed of a gripping and covetous disposition. They had no family, and the man's affections turned so much on saving, that it was only by stealth his wife could afford any little assistance to the pinched and poverty-stricken household of her sister. This, however, she did at times, particularly to Lucy; for the childless woman was much attached to her beautiful niece, and had lately given her the present of a crown to buy what she liked best as a New-Year's gift.

Lucy had not seen so much money to call her own for many a day, as the pressing wants of the family required every penny as soon as it was earned. The crown was therefore carried home, and shown in triumph to her mother, who agreed it would be very useful, but advised Lucy to take it in her pocket to the workroom, that the girls might see she could have money about her as well as other people. She had done so; and now, cold and weary as she was, the young girl could not help taking out her prize to look at it, and thinking how much it would buy, to beguile the way. Ah! blessed power in the heart of youth, to draw streams of joy and comfort from the first mossy rock it can find in the desert of life! Time may have bright things in store for those who outlive the early darkness of their destiny, but never can bring back the dews of that clouded morning, or the greenness of those blighted springs.

Lucy Lever was but a poor dressmaker's girl: yet she found more pleasure in contemplating that crown than many a monarch can gain from his, as she thought how, after purchasing a cheap shawl for her mother, and pinafores a-piece to the little girls, something might be saved to buy a watch-ribbon, or peradventure a pocket-handkerchief, for William Seymour, a young man of her own station, who had given her a pair of gloves last New-Year's day. They had been long acquainted, and report said there was a promise between them; but William had a mother and little sisters to support as well as Lucy, and marriage could not be thought of till better days.

Lucy paused, and put up her crown, for she had now reached the narrow, close, and steep staircase which led to their single room. She knew her mother would be waiting for her, and hastily mounted the steps, but started as the light of an opposite street lamp, which shone into the narrow entrance, fell full on the face and figure of a woman, who rose at the moment from her very feet. She was young as Lucy herself, but much taller, and strikingly handsome, though her face was ghastly pale; and there was in the large dark eyes an expression of great inward suffering; but it seemed past. Lucy was much struck with her appearance and her wretched clothing for such a night. It consisted of nothing but a soiled muslin cap, an old worn-out calico gown, and shoes for which the lowest pawnbroker would not give a penny.

'Why do you stand looking at me, girl?' demanded the stranger in a low and husky voice, but with a manner commanding and stern. 'Have you never seen a woman in poverty before? But perhaps,' she added in a milder tone, 'you also wish for a seat on the steps?'

'Oh no' said Lucy; 'I am going home.'

'You have a home, then,' rejoined the woman quickly; 'and so had I once, but never will again.'

'Yes', said Lucy, alarmed at what she considered symptoms of insanity. 'We live here, and I am a dressmaker's girl.'

'I was a merchant's daughter,' said the woman. 'I had a father and mother, ay, and sisters too.'

'And why are you so poor and lonely now?' said Lucy, who, in spite of her weariness, felt interested in the desolate condition and singular conversation of the stranger.

'I have fallen from my first estate, girl. It is a common story. I loved and trusted, and was betrayed, and now all is past. I have lost one place in life, and have sought for another in vain. But two choices still remain to me, and I am sitting here to deliberate which I shall take.'

'And what are they?' earnestly enquired Lucy.

'The Thames, or the streets, girl,' said the woman sullenly, as she once more took her seat on the cold and frosty stones.

Lucy's heart grew sick within her. 'Oh, don't think of the like,' she said. 'Remember the precepts you must have been taught in better days. Would you destroy yourself both in this world and the next?'

'There is no other choice, girl. I'm starving. For the last week I have sought employment in vain. I have pledged every article on which I could raise anything; and my long black hair, that was braided for many a ball, I have it cut off and sold for bread. Oh, well may the miser value money,' continued the stranger with energy; 'for half the price of one of the handkerchiefs I used to have would now save me from destruction.'

Lucy stood still, for she could not go on. She feared what her mother would say if she ventured to ask the stranger in under such circumstances; but she could not leave the desolate woman there.

'Girl,' said the stranger after a minute's pause, 'you are the first that has cast a friendly look on me; and will you now, for the sake of charity, if you have it, lend me a few shillings, or one, even one, - for one would save me?'

Lucy hesitated. She knew that the dressmaker owed her one-and-sixpence, which she could not get that night, because her mistress had no change. She felt her aunt's New-Year's gift in her pocket; but how could she part with it? Oh, if it were morning, for it would be impossible to get change at that hour; but where would the woman be in the morning?

'Lend it to me, if you can,' continued the stranger; for Lucy's hand was already in her pocket. 'I will pay you, if ever it is in my power, a thousandfold,'

Lucy thought of her mother and her little sisters, and then of her aunt, and what she might say; but the woman's dark imploring eye was upon her, and, without another word, she took out the treasured coin, and dropped it into her lap, and darted up the steps like one pursued by an enemy. Reader, in the days of the old world's faith, when charity was said to be the key of heaven, that single act might have purchased a passport through many sins, and secured the right of entrance for ever. But Lucy had no such thoughts. When she cast her bread upon the troubled waters, it was with no expectation of finding it again, either in time or eternity. She gave freely from her own heart's impulse, and fled for fear of thanks. When Lucy reached her mother's door she found it closed, but not fastened, and entered without noise. Her two little sisters slept in their low bed in the corner; but they moaned and trembled at times through their sleep, for the cold was too great for their scanty covering. The mother sat still by the hearth, where now only a few embers were flickering. Before her was a table, with a turned-down candle, and some humble preparation for Lucy's supper; but, worn out with watching, the poor woman had dropped the little frock she had been mending, leant her head upon the table, and had fallen fast asleep.

'Oh, mother dear, it's late,' said Lucy, gently waking her.

'It is, child; but why did you stay so long?' I thought you would never come. But there's some coal here still, and I'll get something warm for you in a minute.'

'Oh, never mind, mother. I'm very sleepy and will go to bed.' But you know,' continued Lucy, 'Lady Fitzalbert wanted her mourning to appear in to-morrow, and as she didn't know which of the dresses she should choose to wear, we had to finish them all.'

'Then, if I were a great lady, I would pay poor girls something over for a hurry.'

'Ay, mother, but there's many a thing great ladies ought to do that they won't,' said Lucy as she laid aside the last of her garments; and in a few minutes more the over-wrought girl and her mother were both fast asleep.

'It is well you have not to go early to work to-day, Lucy,' said her mother, as the family assembled round their humble breakfast table at a rather advanced hour in the morning. 'But we have very little bread,' continued she. 'Did you get the one-and-sixpence, dear, you were speaking of?'

'No, mother,' said Lucy; 'Mrs Simson had no change last night.'

'If you would change that crown your aunt gave you, we might take the price of a loaf out of it and make it up again,' said her mother.

'Oh, yes Lucy,' cried the two little girls, speaking together, 'and tell us what you will buy with it, for to-morrow's the day, you know.'

This was a great trial to Lucy. She knew not what to say; for her mother was looking to her for the price of a loaf, and she feared to tell her what had been done with the crown.

'I'll go myself, mother,' said she, taking down her well-worn cloak and bonnet. 'Eat you and the children what is in the house till I come back; it won't be long; and be sure I'll not come without a loaf.'

Lucy was down the stairs before her mother could reply, and lost no time in hastening to the dressmaker's, from whom she hoped to obtain at least as much as would supply the present necessity.

'You're just come in time,' said Miss Lacy the forewoman, in answer to Lucy's good morning; 'for we have got a very large order, and I was about to send for you.'

'Thank you ma'am,' said Lucy who, (as may have been observed,) was one of the living-out girls, as those are called who take their meals at home; 'thank you ma'am, but I have not got any breakfast yet.'

'No breakfast yet,' said Miss Lacy, who thought herself privileged to make what remarks she pleased on inferiors. 'Bless me, what an idle set you must have at home.'

'My mother's neither idle nor lazy,' said Lucy, while her cheek crimsoned. The last word, inadvertently used by her, was particularly obnoxious to the forewoman, because a thoughtless young lady, whose dress was not finished in time, once in the hearing of the girls, applied it to her instead of her own name, which in sound it much resembled.

'No lady cares about you or your mother, miss,' said the queen of the workroom, while her eye flashed fire; 'but since you are clever enough to be pert this morning, what is your business here?'

Lucy was young, and though a dressmaker's girl, her spirit was still unbroken, and not knowing how she had offended Miss Lacy, she could not help feeling angry at what she considered unprovoked insolence. She therefore answered rather proudly that she did not come to quarrel with Miss Lacy, but to enquire if it were convenient for Mrs Simson to give her the trifle she had earned, adding that she would not trouble her but to supply the necessities of the family. The latter part of her speech was unheard by any but the girls in the workroom, for Miss Lacy had flounced out in a great passion, but returning in a few minutes, she gave Lucy the money, saying, 'There's all Mrs Simson owes you, and you need not come here again, for she does not like impertinent people.'

Poor Lucy felt that any remonstrance would be in vain. Though insulted, and probably misrepresented to her employer, she had no redress, and therefore taking the paltry recompense of many a weary hour, which was now the only dependence of the family, she went forth to traverse the crowded streets of London in search of employment. Her heart would indeed have found relief in pouring out its painful feelings to her mother; but fearing the old woman's thoughts might again revert to the crown, she determined, if possible, not to go home without at least the prospect of another situation. The promised loaf, and all that remained of the money, were accordingly sent home by an acquaintance who was going that way, and Lucy requested her to tell her mother that she had something to do, and would not get home till evening.

The winter day wore on; street after street was traversed, milliner after milliner applied to, but all without success. One had as many girls as she could employ, another had all her work done by apprentices, and a third never employed any girl whose character she did not know. Many a question of low curiosity, many an insulting look and censorious remark, were borne by that young searcher 'for leave to toil,' till at length she discovered an establishment where her services were acceptable; but they did only inferior work, and allowed scarcely half the usual remuneration. 'I will come if I can do no better,' said Lucy, on hearing the terms.

'Oh do,' answered her proposed mistress, a rather coarse and plain-spoken woman; 'people who can do no better just answer us; and while there are so many depending on the needle, we are always sure to have plenty of them; but remember, you must come to-morrow.'

Lucy promised she would; and through the fast closing night, and a heavy shower of snow, worn out and dispirited she returned home.

'Oh Lucy, child, you are frozen,' cried her mother; 'but did you hear the news?'

'No mother, what is it?'

'Why, about the Seymours. William was here today himself, and told us all. Their rich old aunt in Plymouth is dead, and has left them her fine shop and furnished home, and I can't tell you how much money in the bank; besides, they have got ten pounds – whole ten pounds, Lucy, to pay their expenses, and take them down decently.'

'It's a great deal of money,' said Lucy; 'but is it long since William was here?'

'Oh no, just an hour ago; and he inquired for you, and said he would call again to-morrow, and bring you a New-Year's gift,' said Sarah, the eldest of the children. 'But have you laid out the crown yet?' Ah, Lucy, tell us what did you buy?' Lucy was spared the trouble of answering by her mother's inquiring, - 'where have you been, child, all day, for Mary Jenkins told me that she heard you dismissed from Mrs Simson's?'

Bad news travels fast, and Lucy was now obliged to explain to her mother the transactions of the day, and also the situation she had at last obtained.

The mother listened with that silent patience which many trials had taught her; but when Lucy mentioned the miserable payment, the natural pride of the old woman rose. 'You won't work for that, Lucy,' cried she, 'indeed, you won't and you such a capital needlewoman: they ought to give you something more than a common girl.'

'Mother, they only do common work, and would give no more to any one.'

'We'll wait for a day or two, and look out for a better place. Sure, you have your aunt's crown; and if the worst should come, we could live ever so long on that.'

'I lost it, mother; I lost it,' said Lucy; but the words nearly stuck in her throat; but the old woman, caught the sound, and springing from her seat with an agility which only the excitement of the moment could give her, she cried, 'Lost, Lucy; did you say you lost your aunt's crown – the

London dressmaker's establishment – it portrays the young women who worked long hours for little pay.

whole crown, Lucy? Where did you lose it? Tell me, tell me fast; and I'll ask everybody; perhaps Thomas the postman might see it, for he finds everything.'

Small things are great to the poor, and Lucy's mother was hurrying to the door to raise a general alarm about the lost crown among her neighbours, who were known to be generally honest and industrious people, when Lucy stopped her. It was the first deceit she had ever practised, and sore were the stings within, between her unwillingness to deceive her mother and her fear to tell her the truth. Yet it was not a storm of angry reproaches which she dreaded; it was the reproving look of that sad patient face – it was the sight of her little sisters, pinched and pining from day to day on her now reduced earnings, whilst they knew that she had given away what might have purchased so many comforts for them all. Her, aunt too, kind as she was, was a woman of most violent temper, and should the story come to her ears, it might have bad consequences for the family. These terrors prevailed, and grasping the old woman's skirt, she cried, 'Stay, mother, stay; the money is lost, and will never be found; there is no use in making a noise about it.'

'You're not sure of that, child; some of the neighbours might find it; do let me go and tell them.'

'Oh no, mother; I didn't lose it in the neighbourhood.'

'And where then, child? Do you know the place?'

'I do not, mother; I do not,' said Lucy, drawing her hand across her brow, which now ached and burned between the fatigues of the day and the suffering of the moment; 'but don't mention it to my aunt, and we will try to live without it.' But the mother and little sisters were not so easily satisfied. Question followed question regarding the time, the place, and the manner of her loss. Many were the schemes suggested for its recovery; many an ill contrived falsehood and clumsy excuse had poor Lucy to make in her endeavours to quiet them, and conceal the real cause of the crown's disappearance. At length the mother agreed that it was best not to mention their loss to her neighbours, lest her sister might hear of it, who she well knew, could never forgive what she would consider Lucy's carelessness of her present. But the old woman kept it for a subject of great conversation and wonder for herself and the children; and many a search they had in the streets and corners, in the vain hope of discovering the lost treasure.

Next morning when ladies were receiving gifts, and gentlemen presenting them, when friends were wishing each other happy New-Years, and people preparing for parties, Lucy was preparing to enter on her new employment with the same worn cloak and broken bonnet. There was a quick tap at the door, and a tall good-looking young man, dressed in an unmistakeably new suit, stepped into the room: it was William Seymour.

'A happy New-Year, Lucy,' said he: 'it is well I came in time.'

'A happier year to you, William, with all your good fortune,' said Lucy, as her pale face brightened up; for Lucy had grown pale and thin of late. 'But sit down, and tell me it is all true.'

'It is indeed, Lucy,' said William; and he repeated what her mother had told her the evening before, adding some hints, 'that one could now please one's self, and a man was never settled in life till fairly married. But we must go,' said he, 'by the Plymouth stage, and I only came to bid you farewell. Farewell, darlings;' said William, as he kissed the children, and put something into the hand of each.

'A whole sixpence,' cried little Susan, running to her mother.

'And I have got one too,' echoed her sister.

'Oh, William, why do you waste your money with the children?' said Lucy; for the Levers were still a little proud.

But William would not hear that: he shook hands with the mother, hoped her rheumatism would be better when he came back, paused, thrust his hand into his pocket, and seemed as if he would say something more, but got ashamed; and at last asked Lucy if she would see him down stairs. Many a time those same stairs had been their meeting-place. Smile not, reader; for, whether amid mountain heath or city smoke, holy are the spots hallowed by our young affections; the exile revisits them in dreams, the old man's memory wanders back to them through many changes, and, it may be, over many graves.

William and Lucy talked long together, with many a promise of letters, and many a hope for the future. William vowed to come back with the ring as soon as he could get things settled; and then Lucy would never have to work, nor her mother and little sisters want again. 'They'll all live with us, Lucy,' said he. 'But the times are hard now, and perhaps you can't earn much.' The young man drew out some money as he spoke.

'Oh, no, William,' said Lucy, whose womanly pride would not allow her to accept any assistance from him; 'we don't want for anything, and I have got a new situation. Besides, you will have need of all you have to go decently to Plymouth, among such great friends as I know you have there.' William felt half-offended; but he reiterated his promise of returning soon, gave Lucy a new handkerchief to wear for his sake, and a seal with 'Forget-me-not' on it, which she promised to use on all her letters. In return, poor Lucy had nothing to present him with but a braid of her own bright hair tied with a morsel of blue ribbon, for constancy, which William promised to keep as long as he lived; and so they parted.

Days pass on, as winter days are wont to pass in London, with frost, and fog, and sleet, and rain, and sometimes snow by way of variety. The festivities of the season went on, the fashions came and went, and Lucy

Lever toiled on, day after day, and often night after night, for a pittance which scarcely supplied the little family with the necessaries of life. Often did she deprive herself of bread that they might have enough; often did she practise those stratagems which necessity teaches the poor, to make the shortest means go the longest way; but all her exertions would fail at times; and then, like a dagger to Lucy's heart, came her poor mother's repinings for that lost crown. She did not speak of it before Lucy, for she knew the subject was painful; but often, when most pressed by want, she would talk in her sleep like one who searched for something she could not find, and exclaim, 'Oh, if I could come upon poor Lucy's crown.' As the season advanced, coal grew dearer, the clothes of the family were wearing out, and there was no fund to replace them. Their aunt could now afford no assistance, as her husband had discovered some transactions of the kind, and kept a stricter eye upon her than ever.

But in all these trials, Lucy still had one source of comfort in the letters of William. Pleasant it was to hear the postman's knock, when she chanced to be at home, pleasant to hear her mother's announcement when she returned late from her weary work, 'Lucy, there is a letter for you to-day.'

At first these letters came frequently and regularly, full of true love and vows of unchanging constancy; but by degrees they became less frequent, and spoke more of his own wealth and grandeur, and the fine acquaintances he had found in Plymouth. Alas! the men of the earth are not the men of our early imaginations. But spring came at last, and London sent forth its thousands to meet her by the broad rivers and the healthy hills, and the tokens of her far-off reign came like the breath of a distant blessing to the crowded homes of the city poor. The wants of winter were no longer felt; the children went out to play in the retired streets and lanes, and complained no more of their scanty clothing. Lucy had longer days to work, and the walk to her place of labour was more pleasant, for the cold mornings and the stormy nights were gone; but to her sleep there came dreams of the green sunny slope where their old cottage stood, and strange yearnings came over her at times to see once more the violet bed at the foot of the green old mossy tree where she had played in childhood; but it was far away in the country and Lucy must sew for bread. Summer came with its dewy mornings, its glorious days, and its long lovely twilights, rich with the breath of roses from greenwood dingle and cottage wall; autumn with its wealth of corn, its gorgeous woods, and the pride of its laden orchards; but the seasons brought no change to Lucy, save that her cheek had grown paler, and her step less light. William's letters had grown fewer and colder too, and at length they ceased altogether. Winter returned, and with it the news that he had married a rich shopkeeper's daughter, with good connections, red hair, five hundred pounds, and a piano.

Lucy heard it and said nothing; but her acquaintances observed that from that time she grew more silent and thoughtful, and never wore a handsome handkerchief which they had always remarked on her neck before. 'Don't go to work to-day, Lucy,' said her mother on a winter morning whose dim light was scarcely visible through one continuous torrent of sleet and rain. 'Don't go to work to-day; you know we have threepence in the house. Oh, child, you're growing pale and thin, and cough so much at night, it breaks my heart to hear you.'

'It's only a cold, mother, and will soon be over.'

'Ay, Lucy, but you don't laugh and talk as you used to when things were as bad with us.'

'I'm growing old, mother, and maybe wiser,' said Lucy as she stepped out, for her employer had warned her to come, as there was a great deal of work in haste to be finished; for common people can be in haste as well as ladies.

'Old,' said the mother to herself; 'God help the girl, and she not nineteen yet!'

Oh, it is a weary thing to feel the grayness of life's twilight coming down upon the heart before we have reached its noon, to see the morning of our days pass from us unenjoyed, and know that it can never return. The evening came, but Lucy didn't arrive; the mother sat up, for she could not sleep: but the night wore away; and when the gray light was breaking, her low knock was heard at the door.

'Come to the fire, Lucy, child; you're wet to the skin.'

'Oh no, mother, let me go to bed; I never was so tired; but this will buy something for to-morrow,' said Lucy, as she put a shilling into her mother's hand.

That shilling was the last of this world's coin that Lucy ever earned. All day they kept the house quiet, that she might sleep; and so she did, except when disturbed by a deep hollow cough which came at short intervals. Next morning, Lucy talked of going to work, and tried to rise, but could not. Another day passed, another, and another, till a long week rolled away, and still Lucy grew worse. Meantime, the funds of the family were completely exhausted, and the few articles left from better days had been sold to raise money sufficient for the rent.

It was another night of December, clear and cold like that on which our story commenced, and almost as far advanced in the season. There was no light in the Levers' room; the fire had died for want of coals; the children had crept together in a corner, for they had no bed now, the mother sat on the floor, with her head leaning on her knees, close by the bed where Lucy lay as usual without complaint or moan. The old woman slept, and talked to herself in her sleep about the lost crown, which still haunted her memory as a golden one might that of a dethroned monarch. 'There it's – there it's,' said she, 'that's poor Lucy's crown; she lost it this time last year.'

'Mother, mother,' said the girl, and the cry was loud enough to waken the mother also. 'Mother dear, I cannot die and deceive you. Forgive me that one falsehood – I did not lose the coin, but gave it to a starving woman I met on the stairs.'

'Oh, the wicked woman, where is she?' cried the mother, starting up in the darkness, as if her vision of regaining the crown had been realised; but at that moment a loud impatient knock came to the door.

'Open the door, mother; that's the knock of the postman.'

The old woman mechanically did so, and the postman indeed presented himself; for Lucy knew his voice as he called loudly, 'Have you no light here? Here is a letter for Miss Lucy Lever and a shilling on it.'

'A shilling!' said the mother; 'we have no money.'

'Well, there's money enough in it,' said the postman.

'Money, said the mother, 'is it God that's sending money to us?'

'What's that, mother,' said Lucy, raising herself by a great effort in her bed.

'It's money!' cried the mother, rushing to her child; 'it's money, and you'll be saved yet!'

'God be praised, mother!' said the girl, falling back, the old woman thought heavily, upon her breast, 'and take it with thankfulness, for it is the payment of my lost New-Year's gift.'

The postman, who was in some degree acquainted with the family, had by this time procured a light, which he gave with the letter to one of the astonished children, saying he would call for the postage some other time. But some minutes after a wild piercing cry startled the neighbourhood. It came from the Levers' room – and those who rushed in to see what was the matter found the mother still holding Lucy in her arms; but the girl was dead, and an open letter containing a bank bill for ten pounds lying before her on the floor – the relief had come too late.

By whom it was sent, was never known, for the letter merely stated that the money came from one who owed it to Lucy. The mother survived her loss as she had done so many trials; but the hand of poverty never again pressed on her or hers. Further supplies were sent from time to time; and in the following season, the passage of the family to America was paid by the same unknown hand. There, it is said, the mother has at last found a grave, and Sarah and Susan have grown up almost as handsome as their lost sister, and expect to be provided for by the lady who had brought them up, a respectable milliner of New York, who is said to have been the daughter of a London merchant, and the same who received Lucy's lost New-Year's gift.

Source: *Chambers's Edinburgh Journal,* 1845

2. Benoni's Mourning

In the five thousand five hundred and fifty-fifth year of the world, Rabbi Benjamin Benoni, chief doctor of the dispersed of Israel, dwelling in the Gentile city of Granada, made a vow to fast and mourn two days at every full moon for the sins and iniquities of his household.

Rabbi Benjamin Benoni was learned in all the wisdom of the Talmud. He knew to a hair's-breadth how near a Gentile might be approached without pollution, and had written three folio volumes on the proper posture for eating the Passover; but the principal exploit of his life was the refutation, in public controversy, of the doctrine maintained by Rabbi Joseph Benjamin Joshua, of Malaga, that it was lawful for a Jew to lift a pin which he saw at his feet on the Sabbath Day, which raised his reputation for knowledge and piety to such a height among the Jews of Spain, that they sought his advice and assistance in all difficult cases of conscience, and called him the Solomon of the dispersed.

Nor was the rabbi esteemed less righteous than wise. In common with all his people since the Roman ploughshare passed over Zion, he was a man of commerce, and noted for the justice of his dealings with both Jew and Gentile. His zeal against the idolatry of the latter might have rivalled that of the ancient Jehu, had he lived in an age more conducive to its display; but as things were, Benoni had suffered much and often for the faith of his fathers. Born in Poland about the time of his people's banishment from that country by Cassimer the Great, he had early become a wanderer, and persecution had tracked the course of his after years, pursuing him from city to city over the length and breadth of Europe; till, in the sunset of his days, he found a peaceful asylum in the once Moorish, but now Christian city of Granada. Blameless in his life, and most scrupulous in his piety, Rabbi Benjamin Benoni, in the judgment of his people, was entitled to expect every promised blessing annexed to the law of Moses; and some blessings he had received. His business had prospered in every land where he had sought a temporary refuge from Gentile oppression; and his wealth was then believed to exceed that of any merchant in the city.

But a strange affliction had fallen upon the rabbi in his latter days. Of the four children of his youth that grew to years of maturity, there was not one who cared for his age or loved him as a father; and were gone from him, and he was alone; for the wife of his early choice had died in her summer, and her grave was far away among the hills of Hungary. One was a youth of promise and high hopes, who had become great and famous among the Gentiles for his knowledge of their lore. But he had forsaken his father, and, it seemed, his father's faith also; for he had long ceased to observe the ceremonies of the law, and now dwelt in the city of Salamanca, where he was renowned as a scholar, and much in favour with the Spanish nobility. The other had humbler aspirations. He wedded the maid of his heart, and dwelt in peace among his people, following their path of commerce. Love lit up his hearth, riches increased around him, and men esteemed him liberal and just; yet he never sought the house of his father, nor paused to inquire if it were well with him. The next was a daughter, deemed comeliest among the maids of Israel, fair and stately like the queens of Judah before she was made desolate. But the girl forsook her early faith and kindred for the name and love of a noble Nazarene, and passed her father on the city streets in all her Christian splendour, as one who dreaded not his wrath, and sought not his friendship. The last was a maiden wise and gentle, but not fair. None had sought her, and she remained unwedded, but left her father in early youth to watch over the orphan children and home of an aged rabbi, and returned to his house no more.

Benoni's heart grew heavy within him as he thought of these things in his lonely chamber. Dust was on his gray locks and sackcloth was his garment; for it was the time of the full moon, and he mourned, according to his vow, for the great and strange sin of his children. The evening of the second day was come, the hush of the dying twilight had fallen on the great city, and all was silent where the rabbi prayed, looking to the east, the place of mourning, and the still promised land to which his fathers had turned through the prayers and wanderings of ages. He prayed long and wept sore; for sorrow was upon him, and he found no comfort. But when the last light was fading, there came a low knock to the chamber door, and a voice of earnest entreaty which said, 'Benjamin Benoni, for the sake of Jerusalem arise and follow me!'

The rabbi rose astonished, for the voice was strange, and spoke in the old language of the Hebrews, that had long been silent on earth. Without, there stood a man tall and dark, and in the vigour of his years; his garb was of an ancient fashion, his beard long and flowing, and his countenance expressed majesty mixed with sweetness. He beckoned with his hand, and Benoni followed him, though he knew not whither, yet felt as if impelled to go. They left the home of his solitude behind them, and passed through the streets and gates of the city, and then along a great road leading northward, which Benoni, in all his wanderings, had never trod before. It was broad and lonely, and led far away over hill and valley, through forest and desert plain; and by the full bright moon, which shone upon their journey, the rabbi discerned with amazement the long-remembered features of many a far-distant landscape seen in his early journeys; but the ground was smooth beneath his steps, and his feet seemed swift as the wings of an eagle; for the felt no weariness, but journeyed on with that silent guide leagues after leagues, till it seemed to him that they had tracked the boundaries of many a Christian realm: they paused at last, when the moon shed her silver rays on the spires of a slumbering city, and the rabbi well-remembered the good old town of Presburg.

Midnight lay clear and still on the city of the Magyars; for all its thousands slept, and Benoni's guide conducted him in silence from street to street, till they reached a large but neglected house, whose doors seemed to open before them; and on entering, the rabbi recognized it as the same which he had occupied twenty years before, when his children were young, and their mother dwelt with him. Benoni would have spoken his surprise, but a spell of silence was upon his lips, and he could utter no sound. The house was still inhabited, but its dwellers saw neither the rabbi nor his guide; though days and nights seemed to pass, and they were with them from hour to hour, marking the manner of their lives at hearth, and board, and prayer. The family were Israelites, and oh how like his own as they once had been! There was a father in the noon of life, a mother fair and gentle, and four young children beautiful and fresh as the first leaves of the vine. Without they had peace, and they felt no want within; yet their home was unhappy, its chambers were solitary and cheerless, for their echoes never woke with the joy of the young, nor the sound of festal gladness; there was a shadow on the mother's beauty cast by unquiet days. The children had sad and thoughtful faces that told of precocious care; and there were harsh words and fierce disputes that came often among them, as if the thorns of life had grown up early, and choked the flowers of childhood. But Benoni marvelled not; for he saw that the taresower was the high priest of the hearth. The man was one to be well spoken of in the city for grave carriage and integrity; but he sat amid his household as a reprover and a judge, who had no sympathy with their hearts and no regard to their wishes. None among the doctors of Judah could better interpret the law, and few were more strict in its outward observance; but he made it wearisome to his household by enforcing its thousand ceremonies, and neglecting 'the weightier matters' which his own example should have taught them by the law of love. Benoni marked the canker working its way to the hearts of the young: he saw the dew of their spring days, the keen relish of life's first enjoyments, that comes no more to those who taste the wormwood, and the blameless desires of children, so earnest yet so easily fulfilled, sacrificed day by day to the pride of their father's profitless wisdom, to the folly of his false devotion, and the bent of an evil nature that delighted to rebuke.

The dark seed bore its fruit: the children shunned his presence, and beheld his approach with fear; their laughter died at the sound of his step, and they learned to look upon him as an enemy, whilst round their gentle but simple-hearted mother their gathered affections were twined. She, too, felt her home unblest, and her life weary, for the manner of the husband and father was the same. The tree which she had chosen she found to be a brier. Years of hopeless discontent brought early withering, and at last disease came upon her. She heard the summons of the grave, and grieved not to go, for her wedded life had known no comfort; yet she sorrowed to leave her children, but not to part from the spouse of her youth. He saw his work, but knew it not, for his trust was still unshaken in the power of his vain wisdom and the pride of his long prayers. Benoni grew sad; for, as that fair face faded, its features grew more and more like to those of his lost Jemima, and at length it was her very self.

The guide, however, again beckoned him away, and he felt constrained to follow. They left the dwelling and journeyed on; the same great road still stretched before them; but now it wound away like a long river to the west. Again the rabbi found himself passing swiftly through lands traversed before. Many a stately city, the long-desired goal of far-sailing ships and weary caravans; many a dark fortress, that guarded the boundaries of hostile nations, they passed as the wind in its unseen flight; till, fair among her vines, and crowned with the glory of centuries, rose to their view the city of the Seine. The glare of torches and the roll of chariots, swept along the never-silent streets, as the gay and noble of the land returned from their long, late revels. Benoni's conductor led him on to a low but open door, far from such scenes, in the quarter inhabited by the sons of toil and Israel.

Well the rabbi knew that house and its narrow chambers, for there, in his wanderings westward, he had once dwelt with his children; but seven long winters had passed over him since then, and days and nights again seemed to glide swiftly by, as he and that silent guide beheld the unconscious household. They were the same forms and faces he had seen at Presburg, though changed as if by the march of many years. The children had grown to stately youths and dark-haired maidens; but the mother's glance was wanting, for the light of her love might shine on their path no more. Grayness had come upon the father's locks, and furrows on his brow; but he had learned no lesson from the voice of time: age had only deepened the darkness of his soul, and strengthened in its shadow the love of power and gold. He barred his sons from the love of the Gentile nations, deeming it forbidden, because beyond his knowledge. One was a gifted spirit, strong to think and question, and he despised the faith of Israel because of him who taught it. The other had no gifts, but many graces, and his father esteemed him little, because he had no part in the praise of men. He denied to his daughters the ornaments of youth, and called them sinful vanities; but it was because he valued the smallest coin in his coffers more than the pleasures of his children. Yet he looked in pride on one who walked in beauty; but his glance was cold and careless on her sister, who, though less fair of face, was far more fair in soul. The tares which the old man had planted so early were ripening fast around him; his children already scorned his rebukes, and scarcely heard his counsels, for they had outgrown the fears of childhood, and he had not won the love of their youth; he had made their home solitary, and long habit had rendered them unsocial. Their sphere of society was bounded by each other; and their dwelling was indeed a world to them, but a world which contained in its narrow limits all the evils of the outer earth. The contentions of jarring opinions, the discord of opposing tempers, and the strife of conflicting, though petty interests, banished love and peace from the hearth which should have been their altar – darkened the gray of age and withered the green of youth.

The rabbi saw, and rejoiced for the gentle mother who had escaped so much in the hush of her early grave; but once more that silent conductor beckoned him away from the cheerless dwelling of that joyous city. Their journey was still on the same broad and lonely path towards the place of the setting sun. Swifter still, but still unwearied, Benoni found himself speeding on, rather like one borne on the waves of a rapid river, than the traveller on the solid earth. But now the way-marks grew more familiar; he knew the white sierras and dark-green woods of Spain, and at last entered at the very gate by which he went forth, the lost but long-beloved city of the Moors. The stranger guided him on through the hushed but well-known streets, till they reached the silence of his own forsaken dwelling.

The full moon was still bright above the towers of Granada – though it seemed as if that midnight journey had tracked the course of years – and poured the full flood of her silvery splendour on a solitary chamber where an aged man sat silent and alone. Well the rabbi knew that face, though the furrows were deepened, and the eye dimmed with the shadows of life's closing twilight, since he beheld it last. It was the same he had seen among the children at Presburg and the young at Paris. But the old man's household had gone from him one by one, and left him alone in the winter of his days, like a desert to which the pilgrim desires not to look back; for the place which he filled was the dark spot of their memory. Through all its withering and changes, that form had been to Benoni as one familiar, though without a name; yet now, as he gazed on the forsaken man, the rabbi seemed to be transformed strangely and suddenly as men are in their dreams, till it was himself that stood in the moonlit chamber, with all that weight of solitude and years. 'Benjamin Benoni,' said the glorious guide, who still stood by him, 'I am the angel of wisdom who guided Solomon in his search for hidden truth. The way which thou hast trodden is the path of memory, in which the steps of the aged wax not slow, nor the eyes of the slumberer dim. By it thou hast retraced the wastes of thy many wanderings; thou hast seen the working of thy boasted wisdom, and looked on the gems of life, the trampled and cast from thee, where they lie far away in the wilderness of time. Learn from these things what sin thou shouldst lament, and tell thy tale, that others may learn from thee.'

As the last words fell on the ears of the rabbi, the angel of wisdom passed from his dwelling, and we know not if he ever returned: from that hour Benjamin Benoni mourned no more for the sins of his children, but he sorely mourned for his own.

Source: *Chambers's Edinburgh Journal,* 1845

3. Panhoe Pan and her Seven Suitors

The ancient though unprogressing civilisation of China possesses not only its peculiar arts, but a numerous and distinguished succession of philosophers, poets and novelists, with the greater portion of whose wit and wisdom Europe has made but slight and casual acquaintance. There are those who believe that familiarity with them, as in the case of certain buttoned-up individuals among ourselves, would not repay the trouble of cultivation; others insist that their range is limited to that of the Chinese mind, which never rose higher than the ninth storey of the Porcelain Tower. We are not prepared to put either assertion to the proof, being apprehensive of attendant difficulties, but we are aware that Chinese literature had its authoresses also, though few they were in number, as those of the classic world, and quite as celebrated in their own far eastern regions, at a period when ladies of similar pursuits were still more rare in Europe.

The most renowned name in this notable list is that of Panhoe Pan, whose novels are yet the delight and edification of the more sentimental beaux and belles of China, and have been placed by the imperial decree among the works requisite to be read by all aspirants to the honours of the golden buttons or the peacock's feather. She flourished, according to the accredited chronicles of her native city (Nankin), in the thirty-ninth age of mortal government in China, or about the close of our seventeenth century, and was believed to have been the most learned and accomplished woman that ever appeared in the Celestial Empire, on which account the Bonyas discovered, but not till after her death, that her soul must have belonged to a star that lost its way and fell to the earth, or was one of the three hundred thousand inferior deities condemned to expiate some offence against the great Tien, by sojourning among men for a season. In the zenith of her fame, the renowned Mantchoo Emperor Keen Lung commanded three thousand critics throughout his dominions to bring each an essay on her works to his summer palace at Pekin on the first day of the following year, on the pain of losing their heads on the second, that his majesty might ascertain from their different remarks what was the novelist's most striking excellence. With such incitements to punctuality the essays were duly delivered, and on the reading of the whole before Keen Lung and his council – a process which occupied three consecutive months – it was found that, though not so much as two of the critics agreed on any other point, the three thousand were unanimous in admiring the lady's knowledge of the duties of her sex, and commending in particular the rules she laid down for the conduct of their matrimonial lives. As it was also observed that all the essayists were married men, the emperor regarded the case as fully made out, and enjoined the same opinion on his subjects by an ordinance which still remains among the statutes of the empire; yet the seven mandarins and twenty-one chief scholars appointed to write the biography of Panhoe Pan unite in deploring that no opportunity was ever afforded to the lady of practically illustrating her extraordinary wisdom, and those writers all concur in accounting for the lamentable fact by the following story.

When the 'Disobedience of Goe Hang,' the 'Unprofitable Deceit,' and the 'Propitious Marriage' (productions unrivalled in the proper distribution of robes of honour and blows of the bamboo), were in the first flush of their popularity, the gifted authoress was still unwedded, and residing with her brother Lien Shang, in the second street of Nankin. Her father had been a mandarin of the third class, and held the office of chief tea-taster; but manifesting a peculiar desire for adorning his house with looking glasses and handsome slaves, he was one day found guilty of bribery, and hanged by the viceroy of the province, to the inconsolable grief of his widow, who spent the first year in visiting his grave, selling his slaves, and marrying his children, with the exception of Panhoe Pan and her brother, the former being still a child, and the latter having made a vow to study the divine sciences for seven years; and then the esteemed lady was conveyed in a sedan-chair, with the usual ceremonial, to the house of the salt-distributor, over which she continued to preside.

The seven year's of Lien Shang's study served, as was intended, to make him a scholar of the first class; he received the degree of long-nails from the college of Nankin, and was soon after appointed to his father's office of tea-taster with a suitable admonition against bribery from the new viceroy; but what chiefly recommended him to public respect was the fame of his accomplished sister. Lien Shang's pride in her was as great as the public expected. She had been the unwearied companion and zealous assistant of his studies, and, though something more than astonished at first, to find her genius outstripping his own, yet when her second tale was printed in silver letters for the perusal of the Empress' Mother at Pekin, he lighted fifty-two joss-sticks in honour of the dispenser of souls, and ever after none could be more polite in acknowledging the lanterns lighted on her birthday, or more hospitable in entertaining the sages who came to converse with her through the screen of painted lattice-work set up for that purpose in his hall of reception. But latterly a more important consideration occupied the brother's attention; he suddenly recollected that his sister's youth was passing, and the duty which devolved upon him regarding her settlement in life. There were those in Nankin who suspected his anxiety arose from a laudable desire to provide his house with a new mistress, which he might well despair of accomplishing when a lady of such critical discernment as Panhoe Pan remained to direct his choice. Indeed, the last mentioned quality was the only apparent obstacle to her own disposal, as, besides her extraordinary distinction, she was known to possess a considerable amount of Chinese attractions, in the form of broken feet, small eyes, and black teeth; and that peculiar merit of her works on which the critics were afterwards so remarkably unanimous, had already produced a deep impression on the more prudent part of the community, from whom eligible offers, indicated as usual by blue duck's eggs and verses written on porcelain, poured in thick and many.

The mistress of such gifts and graces was not to be easily won. Panhoe Pan had too fine a sense of conjugal duty to step into it without deep deliberation and inquiry, in the course of which one was found to be extravagant, a second to have a violent temper, and a third to be most shamefully poor. In short, the wisdom which fascinated her suitors was further exhibited in refusing the greater part of them, till, as Lien Shang declared to a confidential friend, in his horror of her never being suited at all, only six mandarins of the first class remained on the family list, concerning whose faults the lady had as yet discovered nothing. The whole family now took alarm; married brothers and sisters, with all their numerous connections, poured in remonstrance, warning, and advice, to which Panhoe Pan listened in the most discreet silence; and then informed them, in a speech of two hours' delivery, interspersed with maxims and quotations from her own works, that if her suitors would assemble in the hall of reception on the fifteenth day of the ensuing moon, and declare their pretensions to her brother, she would signify her opinion of each candidate, and select the most meritorious from behind the bamboo lattice.

The propensity of mankind to value things in proportion to the difficulty of obtaining them has been observed in more countries than China; and this fact may explain why the six mandarins accepted with alacrity the chance of success politely intimated to them by Lien Shang, and only grumbled that the day of trial should be fixed so distant; but Panhoe Pan had reasons for this arrangement, which were not set forth in her oration. Among the sages to whom she daily discoursed philosophy through the screen there had lately come a young man wearing a plain silk robe and cap without either tuft or feather. His face was calm and thoughtful as that of Confucius; but his figure was spare and muscular as that of a tiller of the field, and he called himself by the humble name of Tee Sing, a seeker of wisdom. When questioned by the elder philosophers regarding his birth and pursuits, he said he was the only son of the chief mandarin's tenth secretary, and had been sent on a tour of the empire, the new sovereign's example having rendered that proceeding imperative on the youth of Pekin. The inquirers were satisfied with his account of himself and cause of travelling, as it was generally known that since the late emperor had, in the language of the Chinese court circular, 'gone to dwell among his ancestors,' his successor - the then youthful Keen Lung, whose subsequent mode of eliciting sound criticism we have recorded – had devoted himself to a year of travel and disguise in order to hear the wisdom and see the wonders of his vast dominions. Considering that Tee Sing was an humble imitator of his sovereign, the wonders and wisdom of Nankin must have appeared in his eyes to be concentrated in the hall of reception, for thither he came as duly as the sun glanced in on its porcelain tiles and pillars inlaid with looking-glasses, and the admiration of the sages was divided between the frankness with which he answered their interrogations, and the modesty with which he heard their opinions on all subjects without advancing any of his own; but this diffidence increased tenfold when the lady spoke, and such was his anxiety to profit by her observations that he always seated himself as close to the lattice as possible, and kept his eyes fixed on its painted bars.

Panhoe Pan had more than once passed sidelong encomiums on his attention; he was even supposed to be the hero of her celebrated tale, 'The Reward of Humility,' and Pe Ping Hoe, the only one of the levee who talked with his eyes open, being under seventy, and therefore regarded as unfit for lofty abstraction, had been heard to observe when rather excited at the feast of the lanterns, that her veil was subject to marvellous agitations since the youth made his appearance, as now a hand and then a feature was visible at every sentence. In short, there was some expectation that a seventh might be added to the list of suitors; but the appointed day at length arrived, the household had been for a fortnight previous in the extreme zeal of preparation, and there was a considerable display of new dresses and servants, the former being borrowed, and the latter hired for the occasion, for Lien Shang was believed to be rich, and naturally wished to support his reputation in the cheapest manner. All the family to the utmost limit of affinity were assembled, the gentlemen at one end of the hall with the brother who wore a most self-congratulating look, and the ladies at the other, behind the bamboo screen, with Panhoe Pan seated in the centre, on a pile of scarlet cushions, and dressed in a robe as nearly approaching to the imperial yellow, as legal security permitted, a girdle of crimson and gold, a newly written manuscript in one hand, and a fan of painted ivory in the other; it is also recorded that the lady put on her smallest slippers and thinnest veil for the ceremony.

The six suitors came, each in the robes of his rank, with a becoming train of attendants, carrying fans and umbrellas; and, last of all, appeared Tee Sing in his usual modest apparel, with only one servant following him – a grave and elderly man – who might have been mistaken for a mandarin of the empire, but that he carried an ivory box under his left arm; at that sight Panhoe Pan let fall her manuscript and blushed through her veil. The salutations being concluded and half-an-hour of silent contemplation, as became such polished society, having elapsed, the mandarins spoke according to the order of their application.

The first was the overseer of mines. He said that, being young, unmarried and very rich, his heart was captivated by the report of the lady's beauty, and as he had no particular objections to her wit and learning, especially when combined with such a clear perception of matrimonial duties, he had come to offer her his hand, and her brother one hundred ingots of gold by way of exchange for his sister, as had ever been the custom of the Celestial Empire, since it rose superior to the barbarism of surrounding nations. When he ceased, there was deep silence in the hall, and all turned towards the lattice; but Panhoe Pan, gathering her veil close around her, exclaimed, 'The overseer of mines is a child in soul, his thoughts rest on beauty which time will wither like the bloom of the tulip-tree; such love dwells only in the eye, and is beneath the regard of a daughter of wisdom.'

The next was the comptroller of manners in the province of Nankin; he opened his declaration with a statement of his high descent, the important offices filled by his relations, and the power and influence which he exercised; he then described the cost and splendour of his new built house, and averred that it only required a mistress worthy of his rank and fortune, and having heard of none so accomplished as Panhoe Pan, he now requested her acceptance of his hand, and her brother to name the sum he would require in her stead. 'Pride is the beginning of all crime,' responded the lady; 'the love of a vain man tends only to his fancied glory, let no daughter of wisdom become the train of a peacock.'

The next was the surveyor of temples; he spoke with dignified modesty of the highly respectable position which the late emperor had seen fit to confer upon him, of his own upright conduct, and the flattering testimonies borne to his character and abilities by men of every class, adding, that though his fortune was not so ample as that of some competitors, he had every prospect of advancement as his talents were known at court, and, being charmed with the wit and wisdom of Lien Shang's incomparable sister, he had determined to make an offer of marriage, convinced that her literary distinction would secure her the interests of his family better than the wealthiest connections. The lady's fan rattled against the bamboo, as she replied, 'The wise look on cunning as the eagle regards the mole. Woe to the wife of a designing man; there is no certainty in her days! Let the surveyor of temples seek some other advantage.'

The chief keeper of prisons then rose; he was exactly sixty-five, and said that, though his pig-tail had grown white in rather unpleasant service, and he had poured out his soul in unavailing sorrow over the graves of three successive wives, yet, having realised a considerable fortune, and being in possession of a large house and fifteen sons and daughters, he sincerely believed from the sentiments set forth in the lady's works, which agreed in every tittle with his own, that she was the proper person to reverence the sunset of his days, and instruct his children how they should do likewise. 'What do I hear?' said Panhoe Pan, half-screaming with indignation; 'the owl saith to the falcon, come and make my nest honourable! Grey hairs should dwell with discretion, and not a haughty spirit; let all wise women remember that he who exacts much will give little.'

The keeper of prisons looked about to scold; but his kind intent was interrupted by the dispenser of justice, an aged mandarin whose spine defied his efforts to stand straight on that important day. 'Excellent words,' said he, 'discover a lofty mind, and know, oh! Lien Shang, that I admire the resolute soul of your sister even more than her beauty and talents, though they rise beyond comparison; my age seems somewhat advanced, I am rich and childless, for my only son hath proved rebellious, and married the daughter of a tooth stainer, for which I have resolved to disinherit him, and who is there who would assist me in keeping the base at a distance so ably as the incomparable Panhoe Pan?' 'Learn to forgive thine own offspring before thy soul is called to account before the great Tien,' cried the lady in a still louder key. 'Evil will overtake the vindictive man, and she that weds him must expect part of his punishment.'

The dispenser of justice happened to be rather deaf, and his request for an explanation was lost in the speech of the next suitor, who held the office of keeper of archives, and had the smallest train among the six. He declared himself unable to offer any more than fifty ingots to Lien Shang, being obliged to support his mother and a large helpless family, of which he was the eldest son, at the same time acknowledging that he had neither descent nor distinction to boast, having obtained his office only two months before through the gratitude of the viceroy, whose son he had saved from drowning; but having read the works of Panhoe Pan, and also caught a glimpse of her once by accident at the altar of the winds, her shadow was cast upon his soul, and he came to ask her acceptance of his home and affection. Her attendant ladies denied the fact, but it was asserted that at the close of this declaration, the lady's ivory fan rebounded off the keeper of the archives' head, and her manuscript followed it with a shout of, 'When will this presumption cease? Well may women lament when she that has been called wise and honourable is mocked by a vain pretence; the love that seeks its superior is a child of selfishness and conceit, and wise women despise it!'

Scarce had she spoken when Tee Sing rose. With his wonted humility he had occupied an inferior seat; but the lady's eye brightened as he approached Lien Shang, and the youth, gazing on the lattice, proceeded, 'Brother of the most famous among women, I came a suitor to your sister. I read her works in my distant home, and undertook a long journey in order to learn the full amount of wit, and knowledge and beauty; all these I have discovered and found them to exceed report; but I resign my suit and return alone – for Panhoe Pan is a fault-finder, her soul has an eye too keen for blemishes to be the abode of love, but when my house requires a censor I will remember your sister.'

There came neither sound nor sign from behind the lattice, but the veil of silver tissue shook like the boughs of an aspen in the summer wind; and 'Who art thou?' gasped Lien Shang, almost suffocated with anger, 'that thy house might require such a comptroller?' but at the same moment the grave servant touched a spring in the ivory box, which flew open, and out of it he unfolded a mantle of the imperial yellow, and reverently placed it on the shoulders of Tee Sing.

'Pride is rebuked by the lips of the son of heaven!' cried the keeper of the prisons; 'sound the gongs that Nankin may know that the father of China is among us!' The gongs were accordingly sounded, and that night Nankin kept a regal festival in honour of Keen Lung, but the reception-hall of Lien Shang's house was left silent and solitary, nor was it ever again visited by sage or suitor, for Panhoe Pan the same night departed to the house of the sisters of celibacy on the frontiers of Mantchooria, and ever afterwards devoted herself to the service of the stars, and the composition of those inestimable works on which the three thousand critics and the imperial decree passed that unparalleled eulogium.

Source: *Hogg's Weekly Instructor*, 1848.

4. The Wreckers of Fannet: A Legend of Ulster

On the north-west coast of the County Donegal lies a small and irregularly-shaped peninsula, known as the parish of Fannet, and extending about ten miles from the mainland, between the two deep bays of Swilly and Mulroy, till it terminates in the north in a narrow headland, washed by the Atlantic ocean, and named Fannet Point.

In her Britannic Majesty's dominions, wide as they are, there is not a bleaker spot than the said parish, its entire surface consisting of high barren hills, valleys of peat-moss or drifted sand, and deep sea inlets, which break its coastline in every direction. Yet among these sands and bogs, hamlets and farmhouses have stood for ages, surrounded by fields reclaimed from the waste by a species of rude but profitable cultivation, which, together with the produce of their numerous bays, furnish the chief support of the poor and hardy inhabitants.

Like all the population of Donegal, they are almost entirely composed of two classes, the native Irish Catholic, whose home is a hut, and whose trust is in a patch of potato ground, and the Scotch-descended Presbyterian, who, at least since the revolution settlement, has occupied a sort of comfortable dwelling, and held a farm, on which the former is employed as a labourer.

All are still fishermen in turn; but the last generation were said to draw other gains from the sea, though town, trade, or manufacture were never known in the peninsula; foreign commodities, and even luxuries were by no means so unheard of there as a stranger might imagine about the commencement of the present century, when there was not a lighthouse on the coast; and wild tales are still floating in the peasant's memory of the wrecker's trade plied at Fannet Point, on stormy winter nights, and the families that by it grew rich among their people. The latest of these legends refers to a wreck still memorable among all the dwellers on Ulster's western coasts and bays, and said to be the immediate cause of the Government's erecting the handsome lighthouse which now warns mariners from that wild headland.

Some miles south of Fannet Point, and at the entrance of a marshy glen, close on the Swilly coast, there stood, in the year 1803, a solitary and antiquated farmhouse, coeval, it was believed with the first Presbyterianism in Ulster, and known from that period as the Manse. It was a long structure, resembling two or three cottages built together, with narrow slit-like windows, and numerous small rooms in the interior, on whose earthen floors and grateless hearths the builders had expended little care for either comfort or neatness; but the walls at least six feet thick, the thatch roof, supported on strong oaken beams, and secured from the Fannet tempests by great stones at each corner, the most exposed windows crossed by strong iron bars, and rude though substantial bolts on every door, indicated that the dwelling had been raised in times when security, rather than convenience, was the order of the day.

The household consisted of the Presbyterian parish minister, his wife, and three grown-up sons, a man-servant who had kept his place for almost thirty years, and a poor relation, who acted as maid of all work, named Janet Dinsmore. That was the family name, and a notable one it was in those days throughout Ulster. In every barony some branch of the Dinsmore kindred was to be found, always occupying the more respectable stations of rural life, and generally that of the Presbyterian minister. It was also chronicled of them that, no matter how widely separated, the relationship was never forgotten or overlooked; they were ready and willing to stand by each other's interests at all hazards; and remarkable, not only for general cleverness, but a peculiar ability and success in their worldly affairs.

Whether the Dinsmore's had originally come from Holland with William's army, or from Scotland at the first plantation, nobody in Fannet could certify, though they were not few in that wild parish. The proprietor of the Manse could reckon brothers, uncles, and cousins, with many a farm among them, and much increased in both goods and numbers since he took possession some thirty years before. The entire connexion, were, however, more feared than popular; and as in the times of our tale, the clerical profession was, especially in remote parishes, less distinguished from the lay world than at present, the minister and his household were strong in their family's character. He was a reserved but dignified-looking man, bordering on seventy, and conspicuous from his yet erect figure and snow white hair. His youth was said to have been irregularly spent at one of the Scottish Universities; his middle age had been active and grasping for gain; but since the Rebellion of '98, in which he and most of his relatives were suspected of being deeply involved, his latter days had been devoted to the study of old Calvinistic theology, and his congregation saw little of him, except in their meeting-house on Sundays, where he preached them lengthy sermons on difficult texts and most abstruse points of doctrine.

Mrs Dinsmore was a large indolent woman, who had believed herself sick, with few and far separated intervals, ever since her marriage. Some said the lady had strange burdens on her mind – some that her private potations were somewhat stronger than those of ladies are wont to be; but the minister's wife did not excel in housekeeping, and was seldom visible to his parishioners. She had been the daughter of a rich old man in a more cultivated part of the country. Report spoke of craft and usury as the foundations of his wealth; and there were tales of a younger sister's rights dexterously shuffled aside in order to increase the portion which had purchased many an acre round the Manse, and given the minister at least the repute of riches. That repute had not grown with his sons; though Allan, Archibald and Lesley Dinsmore were active clever young men, with a large infusion of the family shrewdness and promptitude where their worldly interest was concerned. Their father had superintended their education himself, and even imparted some share of his own professional attainments; for the three could quote Latin and dispute polemical points in a style which made them formidable to both the parish priest and schoolmaster.

The Dinsmores stood high in their own esteem, rarely associating with the sons of Fannet farmers, and paying little attention to their daughters; but rumour said they had a more intimate though secret acquaintance with the interiors of illicit still-houses, and the crews of smuggling vessels, while their father's large farm remained but half cultivated, and the crop was never known to be properly saved. Indeed, the whole business of the household was conducted in a careless and thriftless fashion, with consequent alterations of overabundance and deficiency, except in the department which, for the last ten years, had been almost exclusively entrusted to Janet's management.

Janet was a robust, fair-faced woman, now about twenty-five, whose hands had been accustomed to labour from her earliest recollection. Her father had been a poor and far out cousin of the Dinsmores, who perished long ago, on a stormy night of the herring-season, in Mulroy Bay; and she and her mother had toiled together many a year on the small farm for their own support, as well as that of a younger brother, till he grew to man's estate, and his mother died, on which a new mistress was brought home with all expedition; and Janet preferring that condition to the rank of a maiden sister in a poor farmhouse, became general housekeeper and servant at the Manse. Discerning neighbours averred it was Janet's fault that she had not a house of her own, as, besides, being tolerably handsome, her reputation for prudence and industry was unequalled in the parish, and she was known to have laid up some savings by way of a portion; but Janet was hard to satisfy in her requisites for a husband. Hers was not only a stock of worldly wisdom, to which few of any age attain, but strong religious principles and a high moral sense. So, one suitor had been rejected on account of quarrelsome relatives, a second for embarrassed circumstances, and a third for his irregular life; till the general conclusion among her acquaintances was that Janet Dinsmore had too much sense ever to get married.

Janet had been brought up a strict Presbyterian, and was deeper read in her Church's theology than most women of the peasant rank. But at some distance along the shore, there lived a Catholic cotter, named Tierney, whose time was equally divided between his own fishing-boat, and the minister's fields, where he and his eldest son, Cormack, used to work in seed-time and harvest, when Janet first came to the Manse. There were nine brothers and sisters besides Cormack in the cabin, but not a finer specimen of his class in the province – tall, straight, and handsome, with a look of good nature which expressed his character; for though born and educated in the humblest rank, Cormack had a heart as generous and a head as clear as ever were praised or trusted in the high places of the world. Almost from his childhood he had been his father's assistant in the support of that numerous family; and the young man had grown up bold of heart and strong of arm, to delve the soil or steer the fishing-boat, while among the hardy people of his district, if there was a difficult task to be accomplished, or a helping hand required, the man pitched upon was always Cormack Tierney. Janet and he became acquainted at an early period of her service; Cormack was generally at work in the way of her duties about that countryhouse, and many an unasked help he gave. Janet had lonely as well as laborious days at the Manse, for Mrs Dinsmore was seldom out of her room, and all the family kept for home consumption a species of pride or reserve, which prevented even a relative from ever forgetting her humbler station, so Cormack and she naturally exchanged civilities; and had what his father called 'mighty sinsible discourse' between them. At length, however, old Tierney began to remark that his son rather preferred working in the minister's fields, and Master Lesley appeared to have taken an unaccountable dislike to him.

Lesley was the youngest, but by far the gravest and most taciturn of the minister's sons. Allan and Archibald had larger frames and less swarthy faces – both were bolder in manner and more ready in reply; but in all matters of policy and penetration, not only his elder brothers, but the learned minister himself, admitted the superiority of Lesley's genius, and allowed him a casting vote in their family councils. His aversion to Cormack was therefore followed by an almost immediate withdrawal of patronage from the Tierneys. The old man and his son were no longer permitted to toil in the fields, where their place was now supplied by new labourers. Four additional brothers had also grown up to make room scarce and Cormack's services unnecessary at home; and the young man, little to the surprise of his neighbours, resolved to turn sailor. It was the period of oft-threatened and expected invasion from France; the whole British navy was in requisition round their own coasts, and great ships of the line were seen in solitary bays and friths till then frequented only by fishermen, watching over every point accessible to the enemy.

Cormack had been out in his boat one autumn morning, far off the entrance of Swilly, when a royal frigate bore down. He and his companions had never seen aught like that noble ship, and they gazed in wonder, till the captain, who had some questions to ask concerning the lough and its intricate navigation, invited Cormack to come on board. There his answers were so clear and satisfactory as to win the commander's special favour, and he exhorted Cormack to become a seaman, with the promise of a large bounty, and the more moving offer of taking him into his personal service. That captain was himself of an Irish, though aristocratic family, young, but brave in the service, and still remembered for his luckless fate and the generous disposition which almost redeemed the follies of his wayward youth.

It was a proud but sorrowful day among the Tierneys when Cormack came home with a faithful translation of all the captain said, including certain references to the probability of himself, in time, turning out a commander, and declared his intention of immediately joining the frigate, which was expected to cruise about the western coast of Ulster for some months. His mother dilated in her own style on the 'dangers of the says,' and the chances of coming back 'widout aither leg or arm;' but Cormack said 'a boy might have raisons of his own for takin' to the wather;' and as 'his ould hook had been forgot in the minister's kitchen last Lammas,' he would go for it 'that evenin', jist to have things raglar.'

Janet was hard at work in the kitchen of the old Manse. It was the afternoon of a sultry autumn day, and the shearers had gone back to the harvest-field after dinner, leaving her the solitary though not easy task of setting the house in order and preparing for another meal. The number of wooden and pewter utensils which lay before her to wash and scour must have appalled any woman less familiar with the duty; but, with bare arms, handkerchief laid aside, and gown tucked up, Janet laboured upon them as usual, though her thoughts seemed not in the work. The Manse was silent, save in the sounds of her industry. Mrs Dinsmore had retired, as her custom was, for an afternoon sleep. The minister sat among black-lettered folios, studying the doctrine of the eternal procession, which had latterly engrossed his attention, and his three sons were, for once, with the shearers.

Janet's meditations were deep, but not such as to prevent her hastily seizing her handkerchief as a tall figure passed the window, and the outer door, which in that old house, opened directly into the kitchen, was lightly tapped upon.

'Come in,' said Janet, and the invitation was followed by 'Good luck till yer work,' from Cormack Tierney, who entered with an ill-concealed anxiety in his look.

'Thank ye, Cormack,' said the woman, confusedly, as she tried to arrange her gown; but that expression passed quickly from Janet's sensible face. 'Won't ye sit down,' she continued, 'an' tell us all about yer people, this fine harvest weather?'

'They're all well, thank God,' said Cormack; 'an' a'm here for me ould hook; the boys might want it, an' me far away,'

'Is it thrue that yer going to be a sailor, then?' said Janet, dropping a dish, which was fortunately pewter.

'Thrue enough. Where's the use of stayin' whin the captain wants me, an' nobody else will?' A'm to be his own perpiquil sarvint, and who knows what a boy might come till? There's fiddlin' Brine's son, they tell me, come home a liftinint,' said Cormack.

'Ye'll rise, if ivir man did it,' responded Janet, falling resolutely again to the dish, 'and your friends will be proud to hear it; but they say men can learn wicked ways at sea, and the captain's not the best example.'

'I'll learn no wicked ways, Janet,' said Cormack, trembling with eagerness, 'Goodness knows, it wis nivir the notion of seein' fine country's an'fightin' the French, wud take me to say; but, Janet, maybe ye wouldn't refuse to be a liftinint's lady?'

'Cormack,' said Janet, turning full upon him, while the young man sat amazed at her strange look of mingled resolution and regret; 'Cormack Tierney, I wish you well, and I'll never see your fellow; but the riches of this world wouldn't tempt me to marry the man that boweth down his soul and conscience to a poor worm of the dust like himself,'

'We might cum to tarms about that, Janet,' said poor Cormack; but here their conversation was cut short, for, with his wonted grave look and steady step, in walked Master Lesley.

'You can't see my father at this time of day, Cormack,' said he, glancing reproof at Janet, who scrubbed away as if nothing of note had happened. 'I don't think he has any work for you,' he continued. 'But now that I remember, they say you're going to be a sailor.'

Cormack confirmed that report and repeated the tale of his old hook in civil terms, but with the scornfully independent air of one who knew his real inferior through all the chances of birth and education. That was more than Master Lesley had reckoned on or could endure; and, losing his well-guarded temper, he replied fiercely –

'You had no business, sir, to leave your dirty tools in our kitchen, to have an excuse for troubling a minister's house.'

'Master Lesley,' said Cormack, as he rose and looked him full in the face, 'my tools, and hands too, may be dirty, but they hive always been used in honest work; and that's more nor could be said of some people's if all stories is thrue. But here's my ould hook,' and he took the article from its place behind the kitchen door. 'Farewell, Miss Dinsmore,' said Cormack, his look changing to one of deep respect, though the hardly suppressed grief was in his eyes, as Janet cordially gave him her hand; 'if ever I come back, it will be to see you, for all yer friendliness to a poor boy below ye, both in people and larnin'.'

'Farewell, Cormack,' said Janet, 'a'll be glad to see you whenever you come. God bless you,' she added in a lower tone, 'an' keep you from evil.'

'Niver fear,' said Cormack, 'Good evenin', Masther Lesley, wishin' ye bether timpir;' and he and his hook were gone.

'He had better not come back here, the Papist ruffian!' cried Lesley, as soon as Cormack was out of hearing. 'I'll teach him, for his impudence in speaking up to a minister's son; but the like couldn't be done without encouragement, and I wonder, Miss Janet, that you haven't more spirit than to disgrace your religion and family by bringing a beggarly Catholic about you. You that might be gentlewoman, if you would only take advice. Janet, did you hear that I'm to go to college next winter, and be my father's successor?'

'It's mighty kind of you, Masther Lesley,' said Janet, still calmly scrubbing, 'to take such a care of my doings, considering that I'm just three years older, and used to work hard for myself. As for Cormack Tierney, he is but an ignorant Catholic – Lord guide us all to the truth! – but I wish those who know better would always act as honestly, and, once for all, Masther Lesley, remember, I want to hear no nonsense in the shape of advice from my master's son, and have no notion of ever being a gentlewoman.'

Lesley's eye flashed rage, but he made no reply; for at that moment his two elder brothers swaggered in, swearing that they would work no more, and he had no wish that they should remark him in conversation with Janet. Indeed, that was not the only secret their younger brother kept from them. The minister had, for some unexplained reason, probably grounded on his knowledge of their characters, though by no means a scrupulous man, long declined putting any of his sons into his own profession, though often pressed to the step by advising friends and relations. It was now Lesley's great ambition to be his successor in the Manse; and he had been trying many a persuasive art with the old man, whose money had grown scarce in the course of mismanaging years, to dispose of part of his large farm and defray the expense of his education with the proceeds.

On that point Lesley had found the minister altogether impracticable; he was determined to leave the farm entire among his sons; but the family man of business did not despair of ultimate success, which had been rather anticipated in his communication to Janet. The effects of that measure were at once so unexpected and unpleasing, that Master Lesley's interest in, and guardian care of, his cousin, changed from that hour to a suspicious reserve in her presence, and a vigilant, though carefully concealed, surveillance of her movements. The minister's son had little to discover. Janet had spoken of Cormack exactly as was to be expected from her Presbyterian faith and superior education, not to say connexions; but ever after the young man rowed out in his father's boat to join the frigate (which took place on the day following that of the hook), she looked anxiously out on the sea on cloudy evenings, and spoke kindly to the Tierneys when she met them. The seaward looks grew longer, as the stormy, winter nights drew on. The frigate was sometimes seen from Fannet Point; and old Tierney brought back from his expeditions against the herrings, which now appeared on the coast, such news of Cormack as the family were proud to tell any listener. What kindness the captain had shown him, and how the seamen admired his Irish songs; how he wore a clean shirt every day, like a gentleman, and promised to come and see them with his quarter's wages, before the frigate sailed for the high seas. Janet heard all, but Master Lesley's espionage did not escape her observation, and had the natural effect of making the woman attentive to his motions. They were through crooked ways, but not without disappointment.

The harvest turned out wet; the Dinsmore crop was, in consequence, worse saved than usual; and most of his parishioners being similarly situated, the minister's stipend fell into considerable arrears. These family misfortunes made Lesley's prospect of the university fainter than ever, especially as his father continued to maintain the integrity of the farm with that silent determination peculiar to him even within his family circle, in spite of Lesley's unwearied efforts to secure his partiality by application to the Latin classics and old divines while his brothers amused themselves with the rod or gun. Both Lesley and they had, however, other pursuits and associates. Old Hugh, the minister's servant, was the patriarchal but little regarded chief of a family, or rather tribe, celebrated as the MacKearns, who occupied a wretchedly cultivated farm close upon the Point, and had a reputation for all that was unlawful in the parish. Their farm was said to have been purchased by the plunder obtained from an American ship, wrecked on a Christmas night, about forty years before. There were nephews, sons, and grandsons of old Hugh residing in a group of cabins upon it, and many an after tale of connexion with smugglers and illicit distillers followed the family. The former had been broken off ever since the appearance of the frigate on the coast, which prevented the approach of the friendly lugger; but the latter business was known to be permanently carried on in a sort of rude vault, the entrance to which was beneath the hearthstone in the principal cabin; and there were few farmers in Fannet who had not held shares in that manufacture. No church had claimed the MacKearns for generations. The Catholics of the parish insisted that they ought to be Presbyterians; and, by their own account, their ancestors had come to Fannet with the Dinsmores, of whom they had always been the faithful though ungovernable dependants. Old Hugh, minister's man as he was, fully represented the temper and habits of his house – moody and taciturn among his neighbours, seldom on friendly terms with his relations, except when engaged with them, but trusty and scrupulous as a watch-dog in the service of his employer. Like most bodies, the MacKearns had one master-spirit among them. Young Hughie, as, in distinction from his senior, the parish called a short, square, sinister-looking man, whose coal-black hair had begun to grizzle – was the acknowledged leader of his clan, and the humble friend of Lesley and his brothers. Janet, indeed, presumed from circumstances of which she was cognizant, that the minister's sons had that season entrusted him with a quantity of grain, on which to employ his still for their private benefit; nor was the transaction deemed extraordinary. But there was one fact concerning young Hughie that puzzled Janet's mind for many a day. He had a habit, somewhat rare in Ireland, of speaking through his nose, and that in such a manner that made his voice unmistakeable to any who had once heard it. Her sleeping apartment was right above that of the young men – but one being allowed to the three in that old country Manse – and Janet. who slept lightly in spite of her busy days, was often awoke by what she believed to be the voice of young Hughie heard through the rudely finished ceiling conversing with the brothers, on nights when the family had retired early, though it was the minister's invariable practice to lock the outside door, and retain the key in his own custody till morning.

It was with strange terror that Janet had heard that nasal twang in the dead of the winter night. How Hughie got in was the mystery to her. Well she knew it was not with the master's knowledge, for he never patronised the MacKearns; and if at all aware of the private doings of his sons, it was his policy to appear utterly unacquainted with them. Janet had followed that example, as became her position in the household; but often had the woman's serious Presbyterian ideas regarding the proprietors of a Manse and its inmates been shocked since her coming; and now that her nightly rest was disturbed by consultations concerning potale singlings and the disposal of 'the stuff,' as Hughie, like most of his class, called it, not to speak of his mysterious admission, Janet determined to look out for another service as soon as convenient. Meantime the year wore away. Christmas came and passed unmarked in the Manse; for however lax on other subjects, Mr Dinsmore was strict on that, in the fashion of old Reformers; and Janet received the accustomed shilling and cup of tea from the hands of her exemplary mistress on New Year's morning, the only token of festivity ever permitted in that feastless house.

The winter had been calm and cold; but the old people prophesied that, as the season advanced, there would be more than ordinary storms on the coast of Fannet. The Tierneys too were in trouble; for Cormack had not yet visited them, and reports were abroad of the great ship being about to leave their shores. Its crew had led a life more gay than wise under their liberal captain; money had been scattered in all the hamlets on the coast, and every description of company entertained on board, till the soberly inclined of the community concluded that the sooner the frigate was off the better.

Janet felt these rumours press heavily on her mind when undressing one Sabbath night. The minister was absent officiating for a reverend brother, some thirty miles distant, and the household kept early hours on Sunday; but the weather, which had been boisterous all day, with heavy showers of hail, became a perfect storm by nightfall.

Janet had said her prayers as usual, with a fervently added petition for those who had gone down to sea in ships, but she could not sleep. Every blast that shook the old house roused her with a start of terror, for she thought the roar of the sea came mingled with the wind. There was a sudden lull, such as comes at times when great tempests seem gathering for a fiercer bust. Janet had composed herself again with a short prayer, when her devotions were interrupted by the undoubtable voice of Hughie below, exclaiming, in a tone of triumph, 'Master Lesley, an' all on ye's! get up, and come away; the frigates com' up the lough with the win' drivin' her right ashore. Wan sight ov a fire wud bring her on the rocks now in half an hour!'

The words were followed by the sound of whispering, and hasty movements, and then all was silent, except the tempest, which rose with double fury. Janet's blood ran cold; in the confusion of terror she thrust on her garments, and sought a light at the kitchen hearth, for the darkness of her own room was intolerable. Once fairly beside the yet smouldering fire, her strong sense and religious principles, made Janet half ashamed of such overmastering fear. But what meant Hughie's words about the frigate, and how did he enter? Instinctively she stepped to the young men's door; there was not a sound within, but the voice of Mrs Dinsmore was now heard, evidently from beneath her own bed-clothes – that good woman's refuge in all times of trouble – loudly calling for Janet and a candle. Her indolent soul was regularly roused and no wonder; for higher and higher the tempest grew, making every timber in the dwelling creak, and driving whole volleys of hail and sleet against the windows.

'It's a fearful night, Janet,' said she, as soon as the welcome servant and candle appeared. 'I wonder the boys can sleep!'

Janet did not answer, for that instant, far above the storm, came the boom of a cannon, followed by another and another; and she knew, from many a tale of shipwreck, that it was the frigate in sore distress. Janet rushed to the window, and tried to look out through the driving hail; it was pitch dark; but, far in the Swilly direction, there rose flashes of red light through the tempest, as if the frigate were sending up rockets, while the thunder of the waves on that rocky coast appalled her very heart.

'For mercy's sake, Janet, go and wake the boys!' cried Mrs Dinsmore.

And not without dark expectations of discovery, her servant hurried to their door. Loudly she called, and knocked, but there was no answer. She turned the handle, but the door was barred within. Nerved by fear and amazement, Janet shook it with all her strength, till the old fastening gave way, and she rushed into the apartment. To her horror the large bed was dishevelled and empty; and there was a wild waving among the innumerable old garments that hung low in a dark corner at its foot. As she approached, the wind blew out her candle, but under the old clothes Janet felt a door, not three feet in height, opening in the wainscot which covered that side of the room, and left ajar by a hasty exit. Scarce knowing what she did, the girl crept through an arch in the thick wall beyond, and almost fell down a steep flight of steps into what seemed a narrow passage, through which the wind blew fiercely from some aperture at its further extremity. Then fear overcame her, and she could go no further, but hurried back to light her candle in the kitchen. Janet was stooping for that purpose at the hearth, and trying to listen for the cannon of the frigate, when a hand was laid lightly on her shoulder, and rising, with the light in her hand, she saw Cormack, with dripping hair and clothes, standing close behind her.

'Janet,' said he, in a low tone, 'our ship's gone to pieces, and the captain's waiten for me, but ask Misther Lesley for the bag he took from me at the Seal's rock, wid all the masther's money an' a brooch for you in it.'

'Cormack, dear!' said Janet, 'how did you escape?' But the figure stepped back as she spoke, changing to a grey colour of mist, and in another instant she was alone.

'Are they up, Janet?' cried Mrs Dinsmore, thrusting out her head as the girl staggered in, and dropped upon the floor. From that position the good woman raised her by slow degrees, and at last succeeded in placing her where she had found refuge for more than thirty years. Having then vainly alarmed the house, for even old Hughie had not remained in it, Mrs Dinsmore dressed herself and watched beside her servant for the rest of the night – a night long remembered on the western coast of Ulster, for in its fearful tempest, the *Saldanha*, a frigate of forty-eight guns was wrecked off Fannet Point, and every soul on board perished.

The storm abated slowly towards morning, and the peasantry crowded to the coast, but little of that great wreck did the sea ever restore. At day-break the Tierneys found a dog whining at their door, with the captain's name on its brass collar; and from some fancied association with poor Cormack, they kept and fed the creature on the best their cabin afforded, till it was claimed by the captain's family as a memorial of that ill-fated gentleman. It was remarked that the MacKearns looked for no share of the wreck, and were ever after careless and even insolent to the Dinsmores, all but old Hugh; though the junior chief, when intoxicated, which latterly became of frequent occurrence, stoutly maintained that 'Master Lesley had overreached him entirely.'

As for the minister's family, money in the shape of gold coin, was plenty with them for years; but it was said that the servant had, during the storm, seen or heard something which frightened her at the Manse, as she left it next day for her brother's house, and could not be induced to return. Those who knew Janet averred she was never the same woman after, though still regular in her work, and strict in attendance on religious duties. She would spin for days together in silence, rigidly avoided the sight or mention of the Dinsmores, and seemed strangely disturbed on stormy nights. Master Lesley went to Glasgow University on the following winter; but the expenses of his education there were such as to impoverish his parents. He was expelled in the third season for intolerable conduct, and at length became a soldier.

Mrs Dinsmore slipped out of life unnoticed, as her course had been; and the minister died at an advanced age, leaving a ponderous manuscript of deep divinity, which his sons were advised not to publish. Allan and Archibald both married landed heiresses in different parts of the country, and made haste to sell their Fannet farm. The Manse was, in consequence, occupied by new tenants, who, many years after the transaction related, found a staircase and a subterraneous passage, long closed, but intended to communicate with a very deep and ancient cellar, in which arms and remnants of ship's furniture, marked with the name of the *Saldanha* frigate, were discovered, in support, as it was believed, of that popular tradition, which still points to the family we have called Dinsmore as the last Wreckers of Fannet.

Source: *Tait's Edinburgh Magazine,* 1850.

The Neighbours of Kilmaclone, another of Browne's stories that had an Irish setting (1872).

5. Nelly MacAdam

In the beginning of the year 1798, Nelly Macadam came to live as a general servant and maid-of-all-work with the Misses Campbell of Partick House. The Misses Campbell were two maiden sisters on the high-road to fifty, but in excellent preservation. Both were tall and gaunt as they had ever been, with the precise and somewhat stately manner becoming to ladies of their family; for the Misses Campbell could count relationship to the ducal house of Argyle. The reckoning, indeed, would have puzzled anybody out of Scotland; it was long and rather intricate; but the maiden sisters understood and explained the subject when occasion required; and their neighbours with one accord allowed that they were both born gentlewomen.

Partick House was their paternal inheritance; it had descended to them from the Campbells of Partick, whose latest scions they were; but the mansion and farm appended had been leased to a certain Captain Hardy from the north of Ireland, who, having retired on half-pay, and with a considerable number of boys and girls, rented the place, and lived there in free-and-easy style, till his girls got married, his boys got commissions under favour of the French war, and he departed this life sincerely regretted by numerous and despairing creditors. The Misses Campbell could not rent their house to people of inferior rank; it was growing too old and out of fashion for modern gentry, so they removed from the Saltmarket in Glasgow, where they had occupied a third flat with great gentility for almost thirty years, and took possession of their family mansion.

It was situated in a solitary hollow, a good Scotch mile from the old village of Partick, then of smaller dimensions and less resort than it is at present – a house of two low storeys, with small windows and a thatched roof, built in the primitive style of Scottish manor-houses, itself forming the centre, its offices the two wings. And the interior arrangements corresponded with the external. There was a great kitchen, or ha', with the indispensable dresser and wide chimney; from it opened on either side the best and second parlour, the former having in its rear the best pantry, the latter, the Misses Campbell's bedroom; while behind the kitchen lay the dairy, the larder, and a small room thought particularly suitable for the servant-maid, as it communicated with the barn, and thence with the cow-house, so that the outdoor duties might be performed without risk of storm or snow, a consideration not to be overlooked in the west country winters. The white-washed walls, and earthen floor of this chamber, its window of minute diamond-shaped panes set in a leaden sash, its settle supplied with a chaff-bed and a tartan quilt, were esteemed suitable accommodations for a servant of a genteel family in those days.

There Nelly set up her wardrobe and her toilet – the former consisting of a stout oaken chest, wherein, besides her providing of linen, kept in store against the wedding which every woman is said to expect, was her Sunday suit, including the Bible and psalm-book, without which, being a true Presbyterian, Nelly never went to kirk. Nelly was a Lanarkshire lass, robust, rosy, and good-humoured. Her neat short-gown, plaid-petticoat, white handkerchief, and nut-brown hair, always smooth and shining, her fair face, with its pleasant honest look, gained for Nelly the general estimate of a trig bonny lass. She might have been a rustic belle in her own class; but Nelly had been brought up a strict Cameronian, trained to avoid trysts and merry-makings. Moreover, the girl was an orphan, had no relations nearer than some Highland cousins in Argyleshire, and had been at service from her thirteenth year. The Misses Campbell had taken her from a respectable farmhouse, where she had served seven terms. It was no small promotion for Nelly, and had not been attained without a lengthy negotiation, which was at last concluded by a treaty, the special articles of which were, that she should look after the cow and her milk – the Misses Campbell kept but one crummock – make hay for her at midsummer, polish the mahogany in the best parlour once a fortnight, spin six cuts of yarn every day, and receive as wages five pounds a year. From these stipulations, it may be observed that the honour of Nelly's office somewhat exceeded its profit.

The Misses Campbell's incomings consisted of rent paid in kind for the farm attached to their house – which they had let to a wealthy neighbour, with skill and capital to till it – and also the returns of the flat in the Saltmarket, in which a Glasgow merchant had established himself as their tenant. With such revenues, it could not be expected that their housekeeping would be on a liberal scale; but ladies of good families could do with meat on Thursdays and tea on Sundays in those times. Their black satin gowns had been bought when they visited Edinburgh under the conduct of their father the major, who died before the American war, and had required no alteration for fifteen years. Moreover, they had the mahogany which Nelly was to polish; a tea-service of real china, left them by their grandmother; together with a silver teapot, which saw the light only on occasions of extraordinary state, and was a cause of ceaseless anxiety to its fair possessors, on account of the covetous hands it might attract to their solitary mansion.

It has also to be noted that the Misses Campbell were remarkably fine spinners; and practised their art with such good effect, that the dealers in linen yarn throughout the country easily recognized their smooth, wiry thread, and were willing to give the best price for it. With so many helps and holdings, the Misses Campbell did not consider themselves poor. If their incomings were small, their expenses were also few. Their tenant-farm supplied them with oatmeal for the porridge, peat for the fire, and flax for spinning; the Glasgow merchant enabled them to purchase foreign luxuries in the shape of tea and sugar; and a single field which they had retained, supplied the summer grass and winter hay for Nelly's charge in the byre. The provender and the produce were equally well managed. They had their satins for Sundays, and the china and silver teapot to bring forth from the carefully locked cupboard, when they were visited by their nephew the captain,

The gentleman so called was properly a lieutenant in the preventive service. He had been what is known in Scotland as a ne'er-do-weel in his youth. That was passed for the nephew's age was little under his aunts' as will sometimes happen in extensive families, and reformation or sobriety had come with his discreet days; but he was still a bachelor, able to spend more than his income, or perquisites – preventive officers could boast of such things then – and impatiently waiting for the death of an uncle in Fife, who, as the captain expressed it, 'kept him out of his property' – a house and farm strongly resembling the estate of the Campbells of Partick.

Life in the latter mansion was a prudent and primitive business; early to bed and early to rise were among its chief rules of action. The Misses Campbell spun in the second parlour, and Nelly in the kitchen; the elder sister, Miss Peggy, superintended the dairy, cow-house and outdoor transactions; the younger, Miss Betty, kept a keen eye on all domestic matters, from the making of the barley broth to the locking up of the china. There was an appointed day for the putting on of the kail-pot, another for the kirn, and no extremity of wind or weather was permitted to prevent the ladies and their servants from attending their respective kirks every Sunday. The Misses Campbell walked in all the state of beaver-hats and pattens to their parish-church, as by law established. Nelly, with no less regularity, and perhaps more fervour, repaired to an old house standing among fields, and inexpensively fitted up, as the meeting-house of the Cameronian congregation, who regarded themselves as the upholders of the Covenant; spoke of the dominant church as the indulged; and were at once proud of, and edified by, the ministrations of an earnest and laborious man, whose grandfather had suffered in the Grassmarket.

There was little variety, and less time to feel the want of it. Though within a short distance of the busy town of Glasgow Partick House had an out-of-the-world position. Removed from the highway, with no neighbours nearer than half a mile, its news was gathered at kirk or market, for Miss Peggy sometimes attended the latter in the village for the purchase of mutton and like rarities. Occasionally, too, a travelling-chapman exchanged the gossip of the country for the very small purchases the Misses Campbell made. There were, besides, half-yearly visits to Glasgow, for the purpose of collecting what the ladies called their rents. But their chief source of intelligence concerning the great world was Captain Campbell, who, being stationed at Greenock, usually visited his aunts about once a quarter.

His coming created a mighty sensation in that quiet household. The state bedroom – the only one in use in the second storey – was opened and aired for his reception; the china was brought out, the teapot exhibited, the best parlour put in occupation; and Miss Hamilton, a maiden lady of family almost equal to their own, and with something in the Glasgow bank, was invited from her house in Partick to take tea, and be seen home by the gallant captain, whose designs in that quarter his aunts considered very discreet. It was their fashionable season. Yet the captain's visit had a very unlucky effect. He brought them such terrible disclosures of the state of the times, how the French were overrunning the world, and would certainly invade Scotland – how the Irish were in rebellion, and the Papists were determined to extirpate the Protestants – and what villainous intentions the radicals of Glasgow had against all loyal subjects and people of good family, that the poor sisters felt not only the silver teapot but their own lives in danger; and they kept a double watch, after the captain's departure, on the doors and windows of their solitary house, which neither chapman nor beggar was permitted to enter on any pretext.

Nelly had the smallest share of these terrors. Her work was heavier, and her slumber sounder, yet she never concluded operations for the day without seeing that the outer door of the cow-house – the most accessible point in the rear of the mansion – was securely bolted with two strong iron bars, which made it fast above and below.

Nelly, as well as her employers, was most particular about this duty when the long winter nights set in. Her service at Partick House had commenced in the spring; but the spring had worn into summer, and the summer into harvest, the hay had been made and gathered in, the dairy duties had been done to Miss Peggy's satisfaction, Miss Betty was well pleased with her polishing the mahogany, and her execution of the six cuts, and she had been re-engaged at the November term. The captain paid one of his alarming visits the month after. He came in the middle of the week, remained till Saturday, and promised to return on the following Friday, as a particular business called him to Edinburgh; but never were the captain's tales more full of terror, and he specially dwelt on the number of Irish rebels who had come over to Scotland, partly to avoid the vengeance of the government, and partly to combine with the Radicals in their wicked designs.

'I shouldn't wonder,' he said, 'that some of them should be lurking about here; it's a lonely place. Take my advice: if you see any suspicious-looking man, send word quietly to Major Stuart, in Partick, and he'll send some of his soldiers to look after him.'

It was a troubled time; the towns were full of party agitation, the contentions of the Whigs and Tories embroiled the rural districts, and were heard at fair and market; the government was jealous of every movement in the direction of reform; its agents and spies were on the look-out in every corner; companies of soldiers were stationed in every village; and quiet timid people like the Misses Campbell knew not what to fear.

Nelly's mind was full of these matters when she retired to rest on the Sunday night after the captain's departure. Her minister had made serious and almost prophetic reflections on the times, her neighbours had given her scraps of alarming intelligence from the *Glasgow Post*; and the night had set in with a fearful storm from the north-west, accompanied with sleet and snow. The doors were all safely barred. Nelly had said her prayers not without a sincere thanksgiving that she had rest and shelter on such a night; but the blasts which shook the whole house and drove volumes of snow against her window, would not let the poor girl sleep. At last there was a temporary lull, and a dreamy sense of slumber was stealing over her, when she was startled broad awake by something like a suppressed groan. Nelly raised herself and listened. It was not the wind moaning in the chimneys, for she heard it again, and at the same time, a low rustling among the hay, which convinced her there was something in the barn. In common with all the peasantry of Scotland, Nelly had heard a good deal about ghaists and bogles. She remembered that the cow-house door, by which alone entrance could be effected to the barn, had been barred for hours, yet she could distinctly hear a sound of steps and movements beyond the partition and the groans became louder. Nelly was a brave girl, and had a good conscience. Whatever might be there, she resolved to see it. There was a rushlight in the kitchen; and having lighted it at the embers, carefully covered with the peat-ashes for the next day's fire, she solemnly commended herself to the protection of Providence, threw on the readiest of her garments, and stepped into the barn with the cold sweat hanging on her brow. All seemed dark and silent

The Evening Prayer, taken from Pictures and Songs of Home, 2nd edition (1861).

there; but on closer examination, a heap of hay on the further corner was not exactly as she had left it; and as she approached nearer, Nelly's eyes caught the dim outline of a man's figure, stretched at his length, and half concealed between the hay and the wall. Nelly knew that was no ghaist, but it might be a robber in search of the silver teapot. There was no use in giving the alarm; the Misses Campbell would be more terrified than herself; no neighbour could hear their united shrieks; and how many more men might be in the barn! While these thoughts passed through her mind, Nelly became aware that the man had fixed his eyes on her, and was rising, but so slowly, that something must be wrong with him.

'Make no noise, and don't be afraid,' and his voice sounded so low and feeble, that Nelly felt there was little danger to be apprehended from him. 'Come near, and let me speak to you, I mean no harm to the house, nor anybody in it, but I have nowhere else to go from the fearful storm, and have crept in here. Will you let me stay to the morning?'

'For Guid's sake, sir, what's the matter wi' ye? said Nelly, for she now perceived that the man, who was sitting half up, had the dress and appearance of a gentleman, though his clothes were dust and weather soiled. Nelly also saw that he was young and handsome; but his black hair, which he wore without queue or powder, lay in wet masses about the face, which want or sickness had made ghastly pale.

'You're a good girl, I think, and won't betray me,' he said, after a long look at her, 'so I'll tell you what's the matter. I'm hiding for my life. I was one of the United Irishmen, and the government have set a price upon my head. I got over to Glasgow in a fishing-smack from Lough Foyle, thinking to be safe there, but the informers are on my track. I have been hiding for a fortnight past in the woods and moors; and for fear of dying with cold, I crept in here. I happen to know the house, for a friend of my father's once lived in it. Will you befriend me, and God will reward you if I never can?'

There was a mighty conflict between fear and charity in Nelly's mind. Here was one of the rebels, of whom the captain had told such terrible tales. Who knew what confederates he might have ready to murder the household in their beds, and carry off the silver teapot! Yet his drenched, torn clothes, and look of want and suffering, went to the woman's heart, and she answered: 'Deed, sir, if ye had ony better friends to go till, I would advise ye no to stay here; there might be government men comin' about the place, and I dinna think ye could be hidden.'

'Well, my girl,' said the stranger, evidently guessing with whom he had to deal, 'there are two hundred pounds reward for my apprehension; you may get it by betraying me.'

'I ne'er heard that the price o' blood profited ony that got it, and I dinna want the like; but I'm sorry for you, sir, and the night's fearfu'. If ye would jist come up to this corner, I'll gie ye ane of my blankets, and cover ye up till the morn.'

'God bless you,' said the stranger, moving up to the appointed corner; and Nelly saw that he was tall as well as handsome, but so faint that he could scarcely stand. 'For charity's sake, will you give me something to eat? I have tasted nothing for the last two days.' Nelly hesitated for a minute. There was little left from under lock and key in that economical household; some cold porridge indeed remained on the dresser; it was not hers to give; but the man was starving. He joyfully accepted the offer; and when she stole out to the kitchen, and brought him a portion, small enough not to be missed by Miss Betty, the relish with which he despatched that unsavoury morsel, convinced the sensible girl that she had done no wrong. Her next operation was to bring a blanket from her own bed, cover up the stranger with it, and an extra layer of hay. "Now, sir,' said she, 'tak a guid sleep, and the Lord hae a care o' baith you and me. I'll let you out early. But you didna tell me how you got in!'

'When the cow-house door was open before daylight fell,' said the worn-out man; but his tones were already mingled with the heavy breathings of sleep; and after a careful look around the barn, to see that all was safe, Nelly retired to her own chamber.

The storm had abated, but it was long before she could compose herself to sleep, though now pretty sure that there was no danger to the family or the silver teapot to be apprehended from the stranger. She knew the Misses Campbell well enough to be aware that his concealment in the barn would bring down their deadly displeasure on her. No protestations would ever persuade them that she had not given him admittance, and there also lay the risk and peril to the good name which Nelly valued as the jewel of her poverty. She prayed fervently for direction in this great strait, and having thus resigned her troubles to Providence, the honest girl slept soundly till daybreak.

At earliest dawn she was once more in the barn to wake the stranger, and send him in search of another hiding-place. But the snow was still lying some two feet deep; the wind still blew keenly from the north-west; the day was struggling faintly through a grim and murky sky; and the man slept so soundly and looked so tired, that Nelly had not the heart to wake him. Where could he go in such weather, and what would become of him? All fears and reckonings of the previous night again came over her, but she could not turn him out. The more she thought and prayed on the subject, according to her pious custom, the more was Nelly convinced that her duty, however difficult and dangerous, was to allow him to remain. Having reached this conviction, Nelly took measures for his concealment from the inspecting eyes of Miss Peggy. There was a stack of straw at the further end of the barn; Nelly had built it with her own hands; and out of the side next the wall she drew as many large sheaves as left a hiding-place for her uninvited guest, the entrance being protected by sundry large bundles of flax piled up for the winter's spinning.

'Creep in here, sir,' she said, after rousing him with a considerable shake. 'Miss Peggy 'ill be comin' to look after me and the cow; ye can lie here till the snaw and the informers gang their ways.' The sound sleep and the cold porridge had done wonders for the unlucky man; his strength seemed partially restored, and his gratitude to Nelly was boundless. He joyfully accepted the shelter offered him in the straw-stack, and explained to her that if he could remain concealed till the search after him subsided, it was his hope to get off, in one of the American ships then lying at Glasgow, the captain of which was his friend.

'Weel, sir,' said Nelly, I'll do what I can to hide you. For your ain sake I'll warn you to keep quiet. You'll get the biggest half o' a' my meals; I canna steal, you ken; and as rebellion has brought you to a' this strait, I hope you'll get grace to repent, and live the rest o' your days a loyal subject to your king, and mair particularly to the King Eternal.'

It was Providence, in Nelly's opinion, that kept Miss Peggy so much out of the barn and byre that week; the weather was cold, and the ladies had by this time a considerable confidence in their maid. The days passed with variations of frost and thaw. Nelly made the porridge, and milked the cow, and spun her six cuts, as if she had no secret in the barn to keep; but her compact regarding the biggest half of her meals was religiously kept. The stranger grew stronger day by day. The warning to keep quiet never had to be repeated, for he knew his danger, and only crept out after dark, when all was shut up, to walk in the barn by moonlight, for Nelly would allow him no other illumination. She sat up, however, to mend his torn clothes; gave him all the shawls and blankets she could spare; lent him her Bible and Psalm book to read in his solitude; and occasionally gave him sound, though very short lectures on the necessity of amending his ways. As most men in similar circumstances would do, he promised all sorts of reformation, and gave Nelly abundant thanks. At length, in the fervour, he said, 'Nelly, I am a gentleman's son, and if I ever recover my position, I promise to marry you!'

'Deed, sir, you'll promise na sic thing,' said Nelly. 'Promises made in danger are seldom weel keeped; and maybe you would be na great bargain for an honest lass. But I'll aye be glad to hear o' yer weel doin'.'

The Misses Campbell were beginning to wonder why Nelly looked so white and hungry like, when their nephew the captain returned from his business in Edinburgh. He had stayed a week longer than he intended, and brought a large supply of news concerning the times. He was relating part of it as Nelly waited at breakfast the next morning, and entered into full particulars regarding a young man named Gordon Grey, the son of a gentleman of property near Belfast, who had joined the rebels in spite of his family, and after obtaining an ensign's commission. 'There is two hundred pounds reward for his apprehension,' said the captain, 'and the search was hot after him about Glasgow. He was some sort of cousin to your former tenant old Hardy; that is what made him hide in the west country, I suppose; but they think he has gone over to Fife now.'

While the Misses Campbell were giving utterance to their fervent hopes that Grey, with all other rebels, might be taken and brought to justice, Nelly almost danced for joy beside the kitchen fire. She knew he was the man in the barn, and the search about Glasgow was over. The stormy weather had settled into a hard, clear frost; two hours before day next morning the stranger had eaten the last of her porridge, saved overnight for his supply; and disguised in a complete suit of her every-day clothes, short-gown, tartan shawl, and cap, in which Nelly said he looked 'unco weel,' he unbarred the cow-house door for his own exit, heartily shook hands with his most hospitable hostess, made protestations of everlasting gratitude and remembrance – which she cut short with an admonition to 'get till America,' and let her hear of his 'weel doin'' – and departed on his way to Glasgow. A passing chapman, three days later, told Nelly that a sailor bade him say her cousin was safe down the Clyde, and would no doubt land in New York.

Nelly's thanksgiving for that deliverance was often renewed; but time passed away, summers and winters went and came, still finding her in the genteel service of the Misses Campbell. The captain's news passed from rebels and Radicals to the battles and sieges of the great French war. It was becoming Nelly's belief that the man who had promised so much would never be heard of more. The thought was not to her satisfaction; she had not forgotten the perilous days and the restless nights which his safety cost her; perhaps the handsome young man was in her memory too; but what better could be expected from an Irishman and a rebel? She was musing over the subject at her wheel one day, when a neighbour's son called to tell her that the postmaster at Partick had an American letter for her. The Misses Campbell had never been more interested in any of their nephew's tales than they were in that startling event. But when Nelly had gone for the letter, duly read and considered it, she informed them that it was from her lad, and he was 'doin' weel.' The household was kept lively from month to month with those American letters to Nelly, till at length one came with a bank order in it, and she announced her determination to 'gang out in the *Fair Nancy*,' then plying between Glasgow and New York, 'and tak her lad, for he could na weel come for her.'

The Misses Campbell were not reconciled to parting with their faithful servant till the good souls learned, by a special disclosure, that Nelly's lad was a gentleman born, 'but had been left a wee to himsel'.' Nelly got ready; sailed in the *Fair Nancy*, and arrived safely; but the letter that announced that fact to the ladies she had served with so much credit, also contained the wedding-cards of Mr and Mrs Gordon Grey. Till the end of their days, it puzzled the Misses Campbell and their nephew to account for the fact; but when both sisters were gone, and the captain was an old man living on his Fife property – when Partick House was pulled down after falling into great dilapidation, to make room for a newer mansion – when times were changed and the strife was over abroad and at home, Gordon Grey Esquire, and family, returned to their paternal estate near Belfast, and repaid the clemency of government by leading a quiet and useful life. Mr Grey and his lady lived to be an aged pair, and see their children settled about them. They are still remembered with equal respect in the neighbourhood, which owes to them many local improvements; and its old people are partial to rehearsing the singular history of Nelly Macadam.

Source: *Chambers' Edinburgh Journal*, 1860.

6. Disappointment Hall

On the road between Dublin and Naas, and not far from the small village of Lucan, there stands a tolerably sized mansion, square built and new, but so peculiarly situated as to arrest the attention of the most ordinary observer, and few have seen it for the first time without inquiring what could have induced the builder to choose that position. The house rises in the midst of a stony hollow; its front view is shut in by a steep hill-side which slopes up almost from the door, and is thickly wooded; while in the rear, the stable, coach-house and granary, interpose between it and one of the loveliest prospects to be found on the Annan Liffey. The passing traveller who asks the name of the place from any of its dependants, will be told it is Wardsbrook, but should his question be addressed to one of the surrounding peasantry, he is pretty sure to be informed it is Disappointment Hall. It is too probable that the name might be applied with great propriety to many a more stately mansion. Yet the history of that house gives it a peculiar claim to the popular designation, and merits record, as an instance of overreaching one's self.

At no great distance, in a spot overlooking village, road, and river, there stands a small but pretty house, with a green in front and a garden behind. It is called Lucan Lodge; and there, many a year before Disappointment Hall was thought of, lived Major Ward. Where the Major got his title nobody could tell. He had never served in any regiment at home or abroad but the County Militia, in which distinguished corps he held the rank of Sergeant, about the time known in Ireland as ninety-eight, the year of the 'United Men.' The Major's history was not very clear for a considerable time after that period. He grew rich however, and popular accounts varied regarding the source of his wealth. Some said he had found money in an old house in 'The Liberties,' some that he had been a 'United Man,' and player the informer. Be that as it would, the Major had got enough to buy Lucan Lodge and the small estate on which it stood. There he established himself, with his title, his son and two daughters, for his wife had gone to 'the house appointed,' and he had neither friend nor relation that the Major cared to acknowledge, but Captain Munroe.

That officer took rank and title from the Militia also. It was said that he had commanded the company in which Sergeant Ward served, and the Captain still commanded the Major. Blest with a better education, sounder sense, and more spirit, Munroe took the lead of Ward in everything – counselled, admonished, and sometimes swore at him. The two men were so unlike that their friendship could only be accounted for by the doctrine of contrast. The Major was thin, bloodless, and droney – a man of little nerve, little brain, and possessed only of two ideas – to keep his money, and to get more. The Captain was stout, frank, and jovial, bold of speech, liberal of hand, ready to give counsel, and more ready to give help. As a natural consequence, while the Major was rich, compared with his antecedents, the Captain, if not poor, was rather limited, and lived in a neat cottage on the skirts of the Phoenix Park, with two orphan nieces who had been brought up by him. The eldest, a plain, sensible young lady, managed his domestic affairs; the youngest, a pretty, lively girl, was the old man's darling, and sometimes his vexation, for pretty girls will get spoiled; but they were all on friendly terms at Lucan Lodge: the young people had 'goings-on' of their own, and the Captain drilled the Major. To his Commander-in-chief Ward confided his most secret affairs. It was believed the Captain knew how his money had come; he certainly was acquainted with the places of its deposit, in the hands of two embarrassed peers, on sound security and ruinous interest; he was aware of the fears which disturbed the Major's rest on the subject of the little plate and less cash kept in the lodge; but he did not know that the terror of the worthy man's life was that his son, Butler, might think of marrying Letty Munroe, the youngest of the Captain's nieces.

In all his confidings, the Major durst not let out that secret. Munroe would scarcely have thought his son a match for Letty. Though honoured with the family name of the nobleman deepest in his father's debt, there was nothing particularly shining about the young man. He had been brought up to do nothing and he did it; played the flute; played the fool sometimes, as most men do; made great efforts to be a gentleman; made very sincere though frightened love to Letty Munroe; and lived in hope of the time when the old man's departure from this earthly stage would leave him master of the property, out of which he could not always get a decent suit without severe reflections on his extravagance. To leave that son lands and thousands, to see him married to a real lady, with a dowry proportioned to her rank, was the dream and ambition of the Major's days. Letty Munroe's family was not sufficiently distinguished; what was worse, he knew she had no fortune. The Captain had been too easy and liberal to lay by anything for his girls, as he called them; indeed the family income was but small, and its wants many; but the Captain was proud, and had he guessed that the son courted, and the father disapproved, there would have been a speedy end of all friendly relations with the Lodge. Munroe's friendship was more than the Major could spare. He had been drilled, counselled, and comforted under all his fears of losing, for so many years, by the sturdy Captain, that nothing but the prospect of large and immediate gains, which would have made Ward do anything, could induce him to put their connexion in jeopardy.

Such was the state of affairs, when the Southern and Western Railway, which now connects Dublin and Cork, and carries passengers through some of the finest scenery in Ireland, was projected, and Lady Dunlievay came to spend the summer at Strawberry Bank, a handsome country house in the Major's vicinity. Lady Dunlievay was one of the Dublin gentry. The late Sir Robert had left her a considerable stake in the Leinster Bank, and an only daughter, Miss Livinia, who had reigned the belle of Merrion-square for three complete seasons. Besides standing high in the ranks of fashion, her Ladyship was believed to have a keen eye to business, and be deeply concerned as an extensive shareholder in the projected railway.

Miss Livinia was decidedly a fine girl, handsome, gay, and a bit of a coquette. In one of her rides abroad, the morning breeze chanced to blow an ill-secured feather out of the young lady's hat, and Butler Ward, being on his way to Park Cottage, picked up and presented it to the fair equestrian with all the grace he could command. To do Butler justice, that was not much, but he got a shower of thanks and smiles, and a wave of the small and elegantly gloved hand as Miss Livinia trotted away. It must have been his evil genius that brought the Major to his own parlour window at that particular minute; he saw the feather picked up, the smiles bestowed, the hand waved, and it entered into the old man's brain – the powers of folly know how – that Miss Livinia Dunlievay would be a desirable match for his Butler.

Nobody was permitted to guess the birth of that idea, but henceforth Major Ward cultivated his fashionable neighbours by all the means in his power. He made kind inquiries after the lady's health at their passing servants. He offered his grounds for walks, rides and picnics. He sent from his garden presents of whatever was known to be scarce at Strawberry Bank, and, as a matter of course, the Major's politeness was acknowledged. Lady Dunlievay would have as soon thought of marrying her daughter to the coachman as to his son and heir; Miss Livinia had as much fancy for the old gardener; but neither mother nor daughter guessed the cause of their neighbour's courteous attentions. Such civilities are not rare in St Patrick's Isle, particularly where ladies are concerned, so the Major and the Dunlievays were soon on as friendly terms as their respective positions would allow. Butler, like all the rest of the world, was kept in utter ignorance of the great design. That he was a foolish boy was one of his father's fundamental maxims, and the young man was to be enlightened on his good fortune only when the Major had fully prepared the way.

Meantime the railway was also in the course of preparation. A company of wealth and influence proportioned to the undertaking had been formed; surveyors were employed to take levels, engineers to make estimates; the usual machinery for getting the bill through Parliament was set in motion; and the usual ferment about rights of way, rights of property, and vested interests, began to rise. Among all the objectors there was none stronger than Major Ward, when, from the very window through which that great matrimonial project had flashed on his mind, he beheld the surveyors in full operation along a stony hollow which he had thought of planting with young ash trees, but the nurseryman and he could not agree about their price. On inquiry at these invaders he learned that the railway was to pass over that ground; it presented the fewest engineering difficulties in the opinion of their principal, and of course the company would pay according to Act of Parliament. If the surveyors were not deafened by the storm of grief and indignation with which the owner of the stony hollow assailed them on receipt of this intelligence, it must have been that habit had hardened their ears against such attacks. That was the most valuable part of the Major's property; he had a sentimental affection for it which money could not compensate. The company might buy all the rest of his land, and his house if they pleased, but with that chosen spot he would part on no terms.

When the friends next met, Ward was occupied with a different subject; Lucan Lodge was too small for his family; Captain Munroe knew he had money enough to build a better house; where was the use in gathering and holding all his days, as the Captain had often told him? He could raise a few thousands any day on Lord —'s bond; and if he did not begin to build soon there would be little time for him in his new house; but it would do for Butler. Once more Captain Munroe brought up the heavy artillery of his wisdom and turned it full upon the Major. What business had he for a new house? Lucan Lodge was large enough for him and Butler too. Of course the girls expected to get married, and his money would be better employed in giving them handsome portions to secure settlements – for he knew they were no beauties – than on walls and windows which might not please him when they were built. According to custom the Captain did not spare for calling fools and asses; but for the first time in his life Ward was resolute, and stuck to his own counsel. Build he would, in spite of all opposition. His son and daughters in vain protested that the Lodge was large enough, and they would never be as comfortable in a new house. The Captain in vain pointed out the cost of the undertaking; the tricks of architects, masons, and carpenters, and the amount to which he would be fleeced; still Ward held out, till his ancient commander finding his long-established authority actually set at nought, lost patience and temper, applied some parting epithets savouring more of rage than friendship, and retired to Park Cottage, where he laid strict commands on both his nieces to eschew Lucan Lodge, and prophesied all manner of want and woe to its inhabitants.

Strange to say, the Major laid a similar injunction on his household. It was a complete revolution in their history. The Munroes were henceforth to live without the Wards, and the Wards without the Munroes; yet everybody went about their own business with tolerable convenience; only in their respective dwellings, it was remarked that Butler was out of sorts, and Letty out of spirits. There was almost five miles between the Lodge and the cottage, and diplomatic relations being thus suspended, the two great powers remained apart, without so much as sending an envoy, for three consecutive weeks, when Butler's well known knock was heard at the cottage door one evening. Letty flew to open it, and at once complied with his request to see the Captain by ushering him into the parlour where the family sat at tea. The young man's troubled look had gone to Letty's heart; she naturally set it down to their separation; but, as sometimes happens even to lovers, Butler had a far different cause of disquiet, which he revealed without further parley.

'I beg your pardon, Captain Munroe, but my father is gone mad. Where do you think he is building his new house? In the very middle of the stony hollow he wanted to plant with young ashes. The front of it will face nothing in the world but the side of the steep gray hill. There is no ground for a decent lawn, and such a fine prospect lost behind the yards and offices. We all talked to him till our tongues were tired, but it was of on use. There he would build, and nowhere else. Captain, I am sure something must have come over him, he is scattering his money like the sands of the sea, and who has he got for an architect but Grogan, the greatest knave in Dublin, only he can work at a minute's warning, and that pleases the old man, for he is in a wonderful hurry with the house; the walls are rising fast, he is making the mason's work double tides, and says he will have it finished and us all in by Martinmas.'

The Captain had listened in silent dismay. That his old friend was building a house in the stony hollow, employing Grogan, and, above all, scattering his money like the sands of the sea, appeared to him conclusive evidence of insanity. At first he thought of recommending two doctors and a strait waistcoat, but, on further reflection, such violent measures did not seem advisable. He told Butler that it was his opinion there was something decidedly wrong with the Major, and it all came of not taking good advice; but he was sorry for the family and would come over to-morrow to reason with the old man. Butler stayed for the rest of the evening, and gave fuller information concerning his father's unsoundness, the haste of his building, the large size of the house, the scattering of his money etc, over which grievous signs the Captain and his nieces lamented; but one particular was confided to Letty's ear alone, when he stood at the door to admire the beautiful night at his departure, and that was, that the old man always bid him hold his tongue, for that house would make a man of him, and did he not see how Miss Livinia Dunlievay looked at it as she rode by?

True to his promise, the Captain appeared at Lucan Lodge next morning, and found its master overseeing his works, in the stony hollow. If Butler's account had astonished him overnight, the worthy captain now stood aghast at the size, position, and probable cost of his friend's house. Nothing but the steep side of the gray hill ever could be seen from its front windows. No earthly power could make lawn or garden of the surrounding soil; while the yards and offices, which were already planned, shut out a view of broad river, green plantation, and richly cultivated farm.

'You must be mad, Ward, to build in such a place as this!' was the first salutation to the Major, and the attack was followed up with an abundance of sound reasoning and a considerable sprinkling of abuse. Neither had the slightest effect on the obstinate Ward. Let him alone; he knew what he was about, as well as any man in Leinster. Everybody had their taste! And that was his. He did not care for fine views; lawns and gardens were costly to keep in repair. Captain Munroe would see the wisdom of building there yet; at any rate, he would spend his own money as he liked, and those who were not pleased with the house, might go by. There was nothing for it but to leave him to his own devices, which after promising the Major a place in either bedlam or the workhouse, Captain Munroe did; told the young people that he was sorry for them, and they would always be welcome at the cottage; though, of course, neither he nor his girls could come to the Lodge more.

Major Ward's house progressed, and became the talk of the surrounding country. Everybody agreed the old man had gone mad; many quoted the proverb concerning ill-gotten wealth; but there were neither men nor money spared on the fabric. The walls rose; the roof was put on; carpenters, glaziers, and painters, were busy about it. There was every prospect of the house being finished, if not dry, at Martinmas; when town and country got a new topic; for the railway company and their chief engineer fell out regarding estimates, and the dispute was ended by the scientific gentleman's resignation, and another taking the line in hand.

As new laws come with new kings, all the surrounding proprietors were once more up in arms regarding the changes which rumour said the new engineer would make in his predecessor's plans. Those who had no property, advised and discussed; but there were two gentlemen who took no part in the matter – one was the Major, entirely occupied with his house; and the other was his son, entirely occupied with his secret suit to Letty Munroe. Butler had availed himself of the welcome at the cottage; but, as the mansion rose, his father's hints concerning the man he was to be made and the connexion he might hope to form, became more plain and frequent, and were duly imparted to Letty. The pair had nothing to do, nothing to think about but each other, and, under these peculiar circumstances, Pyramus made it plain to Thisbe, that as his father had gone mad and made his house in the stony hollow, his next attempt would be to marry him to Miss Dunlievay, or some other lady, which Butler did not doubt might be effected, and the best thing they could do was to defeat such wicked designs by an immediate elopement. Elope accordingly, they did, one autumn evening, in a post-chaise provided for that purpose, to the house of Butler's grand-aunt, Mrs Dorothea Day, who dwelt in Cork-street, and prudently sent intimation of their arrival to Captain Munroe.

Butler Ward acts the gallant – taken from The Welcome Guest *(1861–2).*

The Captain was getting ready his jaunting-car, and his pistols to shoot Butler and bring home Letty, about ten the same night, when the cottage door, which happened to be unlatched, was burst in by Major Ward, tearing his hair, wringing his hands, and shrieking, that he was ruined.

'What do you mean, you old villain?' cried the Captain. 'Don't you think my niece good enough for your son's master?'

'I don't care about sons or daughters,' responded Ward, with another pull at his own hair. 'I tell you, I am ruined! There's three thousand pounds sunk in that cursed hollow on stone and lime, and God knows what's to pay for timber and carpenters, and that ruffian of an engineer has moved the railway line a mile off! I'll never get back my money!'

Captain Munroe and his entire household were so engrossed with bringing the Major to his senses, that the run-away pair was permitted to remain at the house of Mrs Dorothea undisturbed, till, through her friendly interference and the events of the time, they were brought home and married with all the proprieties. It is said that the curses bestowed by Ward on the surveyors, in whose testimony concerning the stony hollow, he had put such faith, were dreadful beyond the wont of maledictions. The loss incurred by his singular speculation was believed to have shortened the old man's days, and the house remained unfinished till after his death. It has since been occupied by sundry tenants, to whom a low rent, makes up for the disadvantages of position; and, in spite of family efforts to give it a more inviting title, the country people know the mansion as Disappointment Hall.

Source: *The Welcome Guest,* 1861-2

7. The Forgotten Chest

It was the second day of the year 1775. A dense cold fog overhung the town of Lancaster, making its light like that of a murky evening, though it was yet early in the afternoon. Three men sat, with wax candles, and a fast shut door, in the private parlour of the White Rose tavern, an old-fashioned, but highly respectable house at the foot of the High Street. At that period, men of business, and of the most sober and temperate habits, were accustomed to talk over and settle important affairs at some chosen tavern, especially in provincial towns, where the coffee-houses which served for similar purposes in London, did not yet exist.

The three who sat together in that private parlour had something more than common to talk over and settle; one would have known it by their faces and the papers that lay before them on the table; yet they were three as unlike in appearance and manner as ever business united in close council. The eldest was a man of sixty, hale, upright and sturdy, with a look at once serious, honest and intelligent; everything to do with him betokened the well-to-do but not wealthy citizen; and his grey hair, worn without powder, his broad-brimmed hat and suit of sober drab, pointed him out in that age of gaily dressing men, as one of the community of Quakers, which, though not numerous, had long occupied a respectable position in Lancaster.

The next in years – he might have been fifty-five or so – was a small, wizened man, who looked as if he was always on the watch for an advantage; but his hair was powdered and queued in the height of the fashion, his plum-coloured coat was bright with silver buttons, and his long green waistcoat and abundant cambric ruffles indicated the smart style which aspiring merchants chose to adopt in the rapidly-rising town of Liverpool.

The third of the company was a fair type of its well-descended citizens, in his suit of olive green, silver buckles and cocked hat; he was the youngest there, being a little above forty, with a handsome face and figure, but by far the most careworn. There were furrows in his brow that should not have come so early, and his dark brown hair seemed to be going grey before the time.

'Gentlemen, I cannot see how I am called upon to lose so much time, and run such a risk of never getting paid my just and lawful debt,' said the Liverpool man, laying down a paper which he had been reading.

'A Christian ought to see it plainly, friend Skinner,' said the Quaker.

'Well, nobody can say that I am not a Christian. I go to church on Sundays and pay my bills when they fall due;' and Skinner took up the paper again and flourished it like a palm of triumph.

'There are other bills that will fall due at the great day of accounts, friend. Going to church on Sundays, and paying the pounds and shillings to his fellow-traders, are not all the duties required of a Christian,' said the man in drab.

'Well, I have not come here to talk about religion, as you dissenting people always can.'

Skinner was growing snappish, but the Quaker answered him as calmly as if he had said something civil.

'True, friend, thou hast not come to talk about religion, but thou hast come to talk about the case of friend Cotsford here,' and he glanced at the Lancaster merchant. 'Thou knowest well from many former dealings that he is an honest man, but he hath met with heavy losses in his business, both by land and sea, and therefore cannot pay thee the large debt which is now some time over-due, and thou hast obtained an execution upon his house and goods; nevertheless, as he hath proved to thee by clear accounts his just expectations of being able to pay from profitable transactions in England and America, I think that for the sake of his large family and fair repute, not to speak of Christian charity and the consideration which we mercantile men should show to one another, thou art in a manner bound to grant him the delay of a month, which he requests.'

'It is all very well, Mr Benson, but people's just expectations sometimes come to nothing, and every man must look after his own family and his own repute in the first place,' said Skinner doggedly.

'Yet bethink thee, friend, thy firm is but young in the west country; it will not raise its character among men of business to hear said that thou wast harsh and hard with a good customer in his days of difficulty.'

The Quaker had struck the right chord at last.

'I am sure that I should not wish to be hard with any man, and much less with Mr Cotsford, if he had any security to offer;' and Skinner looked keenly at the two.

'I will be his security,' said Benson. 'Yes;' and his serious face relaxed almost to a laugh at the Liverpool man's delighted surprise – 'I, Daniel Benson, will stand security for David Cotsford, that if he cannot pay thee in full, or in good part, at the end of a month, reckoned from this day, he will give thee up peaceable possession of his house and goods, without subtracting anything by which thy claim might be satisfied.'

Cotsford had been sitting with his head slightly bent, and his face schooled to composure, like a man who could have spoken for another, but not for himself. Now he sprang from his chair, and grasped Benson's hand, saying with a gasp, 'God bless you for that, though I could never have asked it.'

'God bless thee also, friend,' said the Quaker, in his usual quiet and serious tone, 'with the blessing that maketh rich and addeth no sorrow; but sit down and let us settle this matter, for well I know that thou wouldst have done as much for me.'

'Your word is as good as any other man's bond, Mr Benson,' said Skinner, endeavouring to look generously trusting, as befitting the occasion; but you will not hesitate to give me your security in writing, I suppose? It is merely to satisfy my Liverpool friends, you know.'

'It is well to satisfy thy friends and also thyself.' The Quaker took pen and paper, which lay conveniently on the table, as he spoke, and in a few minutes wrote and signed a note of security for David Cotsford, which, though wanting in some legal formalities, was held sufficient by the sharp-sighted creditor, who well knew the man with whom he had to do.

'I am sure there is nobody more pleased than myself, Mr Cotsford, that your good friend has put it in my power to give you a month's time. I hope it will be of service to you; and to show that we are all friends, I don't mind standing my share of a quart of claret; it is good at this house, I am told.'

'I am much obliged to you for the month, sir; but I have pressing business at home, and must say good-day,' said Cotsford.

'I never take wine or strong drink, friend; and as our business is finished, I wish thee a good evening,' said the Quaker, as he took the arm of the man he had stood by so nobly, and walked out of the White Rose.

The time would have been when Daniel Benson's family would have found it hard to believe that he should one day act as a friend in need to the head of the house of Cotsford. Though always respectable in circumstances as well as in character, the Bensons had never occupied the same leading position which the Cotsford firm, from father to son, maintained in the old provincial town. Its principal merchants dealing in silk and linen, the two great branches of drapery in their times, their warehouse was reckoned among the sights of the town for size and accommodation. County families and even strangers were in the habit of depositing valuable goods there, by way of security, as they now do in the strong-rooms of well-established banks; for the repute of the firm stood as high for integrity as for wealth.

Mercantile success was neither so rapidly obtained nor so uncertain in those bygone times as it is in our own; houses of ancient standing, like that of the Cotsfords, were, therefore, less rare; but their long chain of prosperity came to a broken link at last. David, the much-embarrassed man of our story, had succeeded to the family business and honours some twenty years before the date of the meeting in the parlour of the White Rose. The best authorities in Lancaster agreed that he was inferior to none of his predecessors in prudence and steadiness in conducting mercantile affairs. Those who had transactions with him testified that he fell short of no man in just and honourable dealing; and those most intimately acquainted with his private life knew it to be without reproach or stain. The Cotsfords had belonged to that old Puritan stock, so deeply-rooted and widespread in the northern counties of England; and he held fast by their principles and practice in an age when anything but popular respect attended the profession of religion and the name of Puritan.

'The race is not to the swift nor the battle to the strong, nor bread to the wise in heart,' says Solomon; and the text was proved almost to the letter in David's Cotsford's case. Notwithstanding the fair prospects with which he had begun life, his own abilities, and the good old ways he chose to walk in, the latter years of his mercantile life had been crossed by all the misfortunes to which men of business are specially liable. He had lost by shipwrecks and by failures, by the changes of fashion, and by the chances of his time. The rise of the cotton manufacture, then becoming a power in England by improvements and inventions in its machinery, lowered the value of the goods in which he dealt. The American War of Independence, which had lately raged, and the disturbed state of trade which preceded it, had no less disastrous consequences. David had met those trials with a brave heart and a steady hand, and spared no exertion or honest expedient to maintain the ancient credit and position of his house; but the work was beyond his power, and David had no connections to count on.

He had married early a lady whose fair face and fairer virtues were her only dowry. They had a large family, their children being now ten in number. They had been liberal and helpful to poor relations on both sides; to poor neighbours and strangers also. They had kept up appearances perhaps longer than they should have done; but something must be allowed for human weakness and ancestral pride; and thus, between public and private causes of decay, the once flourishing firm of Cotsford was reduced to a condition which nobody in Lancaster was fully aware of, except the three who met that evening in the parlour of the White Rose.

The threatened ruin had been warded off by David's best and now only friend, Daniel Benson. There was an old acquaintance between the families of Benson and Cotsford. They were of equally ancient root in Lancaster. They had equally shared in the troubles which beset Nonconformists in earlier times, and by the reproach incurred by sober and serious living in their own; for to these ills the Quaker was not less subject than the Puritan; and they had kept unbroken the bonds of peace and Christian charity, notwithstanding a difference of opinion, which in those bygone generations made adversaries of men who held fast the same fundamental truths.

The old acquaintance grew more intimate in David's evil days. The misfortunes which scattered away the friends of Cotsford's prosperity, and kept worldly men at a distance from the falling house drew the kindly Quaker nearer. Benson was the only man in his native town to whom David could lay open the whole extent of his difficulties, and bring to mediate with his hard and grasping creditor; and the plain-speaking unprofessing friend had done more than he could have asked or hoped for.

They walked now arm in arm like brothers through the heavy fog and the deserted High Street, talking hopefully of the better days that might come, till they reached Benson's door.

'Wilt thou come in and warm thyself?' said Daniel, as he caught sight of the bright blazing fire through his own parlour window.

'No, thank you,' said David, 'I must go home; the family will expect me by this time; but I shall never forget what you have done for me this day, Mr Benson.'

'Say no more about it, friend;' and the Quaker shook his hand. 'Go home if thy duty call thee; but, above all, put thy trust in Him who hath done and can do everything for thee and me also, and neither fear nor fret, for fearing and fretting much disquiet the mind, and interfere with business.'

David turned away as Daniel passed into his house; but he did not go home, though the family might be expecting him. There was an expectation in his own breast which kept the unlucky merchant wandering about the streets of the old town, in spite of the cold, thick fog, which shut most of its people fast within doors. David was one of those characters that are frank on the surface but reserved beneath it. He would clearly explain or relate all that was necessary in business, or even for the confidence of friendship; but there was always something kept to himself which he would not tell, and that was the something which concerned him most.

On that particular day the Irish and American mails were, according to the postal arrangements of the time, due in Lancaster, but could not be looked for till night-fall on account of the fog; and David had reason to expect that he would have intelligence from his confidential agents in Dublin and New York regarding the important transactions on which the hopes of satisfying his Liverpool creditor were founded. It was not the dread of what such intelligence might be that possessed him. There was nothing to fear, as far as he knew; but a restless, feverish feeling of suspense, which he would let nobody see or share, kept him pacing up one street and down another, till the night fell early and thick; and he heard the bugle blast with which the coach carrying the western mails drove up to the post-office.

David was first at the window, to which letters were duly delivered to all applicants; for the postman's knock was a thing yet unknown in provincial towns. There were two for him. He knew the handwriting of his agents, and rushed away to where one of the oil lamps, with which Lancaster in common with all cities of the period was lighted, glimmered faintly through the fog at the entrance of a neighbouring alley.

It cost him but a minute or two to tear open and read both letters by its light; but there David stood with the papers in his hand as if rooted to the spot till somebody pushed against him. It was one of the night watch on his first round, and the man uttered an exclamation of surprise as he caught sight of the ghastly pale face with which Cotsford turned from the lamp, thrust the letters into his coat pocket, and walked quickly towards his home.

Mr Cotsford's house in the High Street of Lancaster was a good specimen of the wealthy merchant's dwelling in those days in old provincial towns. It was a substantial building of four storeys, broad and deep, with a high-pitched roof and narrow windows; those of the ground-floor well secured by out and inside shutters, for they lighted a large warehouse and other business rooms; while those above showed by their drapery and decorations that they were inhabited by the family.

On one side of the house a strong gate opened on an arched passage wide enough for cart or wagon, and leading to an inner courtyard for the convenient delivery or dispatch of goods; and above the broad street door was sculptured the "sign" or arms of the Cotsford family; a ship in full sail, with the motto, "God is my pilot," and the date 1560

The strong gate was fast locked, and the warehouse all shut up and dark, but there were lights in the family rooms above, and at the street door a lady in a dress which had been rich and handsome, but was now well worn, stood looking out on the foggy night as if for some late but expected comer. The lady had been handsome in her youth, and was still so in her middle age, though care and anxiety, with a large family and adverse fortunes, had sapped her once rosy health, made her beautiful face thin and pallid, and streaked her golden hair with untimely grey.

'Is it you, David dear?' she said, in a tone so soft and sweet that would have made any man believe he was welcome.

'It is, Grace,' said Cotsford, as he stepped in; 'but I am sorry to see you at the open door this bitter night.'

'I was looking out for you, dear;' the supper is on the table; but you know none of us care to sit down without you. The children say it is no supper at all without father. Did you settle the business you went upon, David dear?' she added, almost in a whisper.

'It is settled – all settled – my good wife. Do go upstairs out of the cold. I will bolt the door, and be with you in a minute.' said Cotsford.

The merchant's second parlour, the family room, was a pleasant sight for one coming in from the dreary fog of that winter night, and the hard, cold transactions of business: a bright coal fire and two large mould candles lighted up its wainscot walls. The eye caught at a glance the portraits of notable ancestors or famous Puritan divines, well painted, set in gold gilt frames, and hung in conspicuous positions; the furniture of dark mahogany, polished and ponderous, after the domestic fashions of our forefathers; the well-spread supper table, and the family gathered round it.

The ten children were there – a handsome, rosy circle, that seemed to have taken and kept the lost bloom of their mother, descending like steps in age without a gap between, from the two eldest girls, now in early womanhood, and so helpful to their mother that she was accustomed to call them her two hands, to the lisping little one, who still occupied the elevated chair, and was known to both family and friends as the baby. In the midst of many misfortunes the Cotsfords retained some blessings which riches cannot give nor poverty take away. They were a family governed by love, dwelling together in unity, and making their home on earth bear some distant resemblance to the home above.

It might have cheered the father's heart, if anything could have done so at that moment, to see the smile that broke like sunshine over every face when he entered, and how one and all rose with a welcome. The eldest daughter helped off his cloak, the eldest son ran to place a chair for him, and the younger children crowded round him with all sorts of questions – chiefly why he was so late in coming home, and if he had lost his way in the fog.

David had a kind word and a father's hand for them all. He clapped his boys on the back, he stroked the hair of his girls, he answered most of their questions, he heard all their news, and took his place at the table opposite Mrs Cotsford, which he had occupied, with few and far between intervals of absence, for more than twenty years. Then David said the accustomed grace, and the supper proceeded as usual, the elder boys and girls waiting on their parents and the younger children; for the Cotsfords kept no servants now.

The young people noticed nothing in their father's manner, except that he spoke little, and seemed careless of his supper; but they were used to see him thoughtful and silent at times. When the meal was over he read the accustomed chapter in the Bible, and offered up the evening prayer; and when they rose from their knees, he bade them all, and even Mrs Cotsford, a kind, but hasty good-night, saying he had a matter to look into in his office, and would sit up some time by himself.

There was a manly, yet tender, heart in that unlucky merchant. He had married for love, and true to the constancy of noble natures, that love had never changed through the wear of time and the trials of hard fortune; but he had been blessed with a woman worthy of it – the greatest blessing that can fall to the lot of man on this side of the sky. David had found in his Grace not only a faithful and loving wife, but a true helpmate. She had been blithe with him in the sunshine of his days, and in her prudence, courage, and affection lay the chief comfort and support of his adversity.

David's trust in his wife was only second to his trust in Providence; but he had seen her health failing under the cares and anxieties of later years. That winter it had been particularly delicate and the wish to spare her trouble of mind as far as possible made him, for the first time, conceal from her the whole account of his difficulties. Thus Mrs Cotsford knew nothing of the impending execution, but believed that her husband had gone to the White Rose that evening to negotiate with the Liverpool merchant regarding some additional time for the payment of his debt.

David had worse news now. One of the letters he had waited for and read by the lamp in the alley informed him that the Dublin merchant, from whom he had such large and just expectations, had died suddenly, and he was found to be a hopeless bankrupt. The other told him that the American troops, under General Washington, had taken possession of New York, and his goods entrusted to his agent there had been confiscated as British property, by way of reprisal for similar doings by the expelled royalist garrison.

There was an end to all the hopes Cotsford had cherished of paying off his Liverpool creditor, and at last gaining back his position. The execution must take effect at the end of the month; the kindness of the friendly Quaker could only give him and his family time to prepare for it. There was no longer any use in concealing the worst from Mrs Cotsford; yet the man's heart, which had borne up so bravely against many a heavy disappointment failed him in this. It was not that he dreaded reproaches, hysterics, or any of those scenes which are too apt to follow on the discovery of great family misfortunes. David was better acquainted with the sensible, pious, and noble character of his wife to fear the like; but he shrunk from telling her the terrible news till his own mind got somewhat familiar with it; and, knowing that he could neither rest or sleep in the present condition of his thoughts, David made a pretext of matters to be looked into in his office, and walked quietly downstairs, candle in hand, to sit by himself, and look ruin in the face, if he could.

There had been built in his grandfather's time, on part of the inner courtyard, a large room, called the back warehouse, for the storage of goods not immediately wanted. David remembered when there was scarcely a passage between the piled-up bales and packages with which it was crowded; but the back warehouse had been all but empty for years, and now, with the exception of some fragments of lumber, it contained nothing but a low bench set against one of the walls, and an old chest in the corner.

To that empty out of the way room, poor Cotsford retired, to be as far out of sight and hearing of his family as possible. He shut the door softly – its latch had grown useless with time and wear – sat down on the low bench, set his candle on a shelf hard by, bowed his troubled head upon his hands, and tried to think soberly of what he had to meet. It was a difficult task for a man of his high spirit to contemplate the blight which must fall upon his credit, the merchant's fair fame, when it was known in Lancaster that a stranger was in possession of the house of Cotsford. How different was the position of that house when he became its head! How poor must be the prospects of his children compared to what his own had been! David knew he was not to blame for the woeful change. He had done everything for the best as far as his judgement and foresight went; no reproach could rest upon his honour or his conscience; yet men of far less abilities and no integrity had prospered under his eyes; and, as one example of the kind rose after another to his memory, contrasted with the long train of his own unmerited misfortunes, it seemed that the faith and hope of his Puritan fathers, which had strengthened their hearts through trying and troubled times, was failing him at last, and he was ready to say, like the men of Israel, 'What profit is there that we have served the Lord?'

Lost in these lonely musings, Cotsford did not hear the unlatched door softly opened, and a light step cross the room, but he felt a gentle hand laid on his shoulder, and looked up to see this wife by his side.

'David dear,' she said, 'I knew you had some trouble on your mind to-night. The children are all asleep; we are alone here under the Eye that never slumbers, and, for all the love that has been between us, and all the happy years we have spent together, let me share it with you, as I have shared everything else. Whatever it is, my own husband, do not hide it from me.'

'You should have got a luckier man for a husband, Grace.' David spoke out of the bitterness of his thoughts.

'I could never have got a better. But tell me what troubles you? Lucky or unlucky, you are the only man I would have, first or last, if a thousand were in my choice. Tell your own Grace what has happened;' and, sitting down by his side, she threw her arms around him.

'You will hear it soon enough, my poor woman, and may as well hear it now,' said Cotsford, mastering his emotions with an assumed composure, that made him appear cold and hard for the first time in his life; and he proceeded to tell her in brief but plain terms, the entire state of the case.

His eyes were on the ground all the time and, when he looked up at last, the ghastly paleness of her startled him; but the next moment the wise and loving woman was herself again.

'David dear,' she said, and her clasp grew tighter, 'it is a hard trial for you and for us all; but we know it is the work of Providence, and no fault of yours. You have always done your duty. Don't be cast down. Though all this come upon us, we shall not want; the Lord in whom we have trusted will provide for us and ours. David dear, he has given us yet better things than riches – what they could never buy. He who gave his own Son to die for our sins, will He not with Him freely give us all things? And then, think of our children – so good, so dutiful, so blessed with health and strength; and think of what you and I have been to one another – what you are to me, my own love – more than all the wealth of this world could purchase; and more than that, David, think of our part in the promise of the better life to come. Surely these blessings should enable us to bear up against the chances of time and fortune.'

'I can bear anything with you by my side, Grace. A help and comfort you have been to me since we came together, and never more than now, when a man needs it,' said Cotsford, clasping his wife in his turn; and the two sat there in the deep mid-night, and with no prospect but that of worldly ruin before them; yet the tears in their eyes were of love, and not of sorrow.

'What grieves me most,' said Cotsford, returning to his sad subject, as both grew calm again, is the thought of you and the children being turned out of house and home.'

'Never mind that, dear. Mr Benson's kindness – the Lord remember it to him! – has given us a month to prepare against the evil day; and, if no better can be done, our relatives will take us in till you can find a home for us. However poor and small it may be, we will all be happy there, if you and the blessing of God are with us. Besides, David, the Hand that has brought us low, can lift us up again. You know not what Providence may have in store for us yet; keep up your heart. But what's that?' said Mrs Cotsford, as a sound of scraping close by startled her shaken nerves.

'It's only a rat behind that old chest in the corner.' said David, smiling, in spite of his troubles, at her sudden fright. 'But come away, dear; this is a cold place for you;' and he rose and took his wife by the arm.

'That is a queer old chest,' said Mrs Cotford, contemplating the receptacle he referred to, a square, solid-looking piece of furniture of the make between the chest and the coffer. 'Are there any goods in it? I have seen it standing in that corner for ever so long, and meant to ask you about it many a time, but forgot.'

'There are no goods of ours in it, but it has stood in that corner for thirty years, and I forgot, up till this very moment, that it ought to be advertised, in order to give its rightful owners a chance of sending for it, before Skinner takes possession. Maybe I have never told you how it came into our hands; we did not happen to speak about it, and the matter went out of my mind, though it is curious.

'I was a boy at the time; but, as far as my memory goes, it was the beginning of the forty-five, the Pretender's year, you know, when we and all the Protestant people of the north were preparing to support king and constitution with train-bands and fortified walls. My father had been elected mayor of Lancaster for the second time, and his public duties were apt to encroach on his hours of business, which made him occasionally sit late in his office. I was assisting him there one evening after the outer gate had been shut, and most of the family were gone to bed, when we heard a loud ring of the bell, and he sent me out to see what was wanted at that unreasonable hour. Outside there stood a carrier we used to employ, and so did the first merchants of the town, believing him to be an honest and a loyal man, though afterwards he fled the country on account of business he was said to have done for the Earl of Derwentwater and other leading Jacobites. I suppose he died abroad for nobody has heard of him since. His name was Ephraim Jenkins, and though generally sensible enough, he appeared to have taken a glass too much that evening, and so did a countryman who was with him, for all I could get out of either was, that they had come to leave this chest, which they brought in a cart, and said was full of Manchester goods, in my father's warehouse for a merchant in Derby, who would send for it in a few days. They mentioned the merchant's name, but it was not known to us.'

However, my father was in the habit of taking in goods for inland friends, and would not refuse a stranger that service in such a troubled time; he therefore allowed Jenkins and his companions to bring in the chest – a heavy burden it seemed for them – and set it in this corner, the only spot where there was room enough. Time passed, and we did not hear from the merchant in Derby, as the Rebellion increased, and the town was taken by the Pretender's army, though they did not keep it long; my father thought he might have been one of those who fled before them.

But when the Rebellion was fairly put down, and things were settled in north and south, nobody in Derby or its neighbourhood could give

The Discovery of Gold Coins – taken from The Forgotten Chest (1893).

him the smallest information regarding the owner of the chest. Jenkins had fled the country by that time, and his companion we never saw again; so there it has stood; and the warehouse that was so full when it came in is bare and empty of everything but itself;' and Cotsford struck the mouldering old chest with his foot.

The thought he expressed had made the serious, peaceable man somewhat violent. A crash of breaking timber followed the blow, then a clunking sound; and as he caught up the candle and stooped, an exclamation of surprise burst at once from husband and wife; for, pouring from a rent in the side of the old chest, they saw a perfect stream of gold coins. It was no fairy gold, but substantial pieces, well known throughout Europe of the period by the name of Louis d'ors, and every one showing the heavy face of Louis XV, King of France, whose long reign had come to a close in the preceding year.

David Cotsford lost no time in opening the old chest; it was easily done, though securely locked, and the lid nailed down – time had told on the iron and damp on the wood; and he discovered that, instead of being filled with Manchester goods, it was packed with webs of linen from French Flanders, and beneath them a number of sealed bags, every one filled with Louis d'ors. There were no papers, no addresses to show the proper owners or receivers, but every bag was labelled to Flavius Quintus, or some other name from old Roman story, 'for the service of the Prince.'

This made the case clear to the intelligent Cotsfords; such names had been assumed by the leaders of the Jacobite party in England, by way of ensuring their own safety, especially in communication with their friends and assistants in France; and those bags of Louis d'ors were manifestly part of the funds furnished from that country to carry on the civil war, which was to reinstate the Stuarts. The chest had been sent to the warehouse of a loyal Protestant merchant for safe keeping, till the traitorous agents found a fitting opportunity to remove it; for no one would look for anything of the sort there. The opportunity had never been found; the cause had been hopelessly defeated; the grave had closed over most of the generation engaged for or against it, and the chest, with its hidden gold, had remained all those long years in the corner of David Cotsford's warehouse, to be discovered at last by what seemed the merest accident, and relieved the honest man, so sorely tried by misfortune, from all his danger and difficulty.

David and his wife were both blessed with prudence and understanding; their children being all asleep at the time of the discovery, the secret remained between themselves and Daniel Benson, to whom as their best, and most trusty friend, they told it. With his assistance, Cotsford managed to pay the Liverpool merchant and all his other creditors, and retrieve his position among the leading men of Lancaster, in a manner which attracted no suspicion. People only said that the tide had turned with him at last, as they always knew it would; but partly his ill-success in his hereditary business, partly the amount of foreign money he had to dispose of, made him determine to give up merchandise and become a banker. By this step he was enabled to further the fortunes of his faithful friend, for Daniel Benson became his partner, and the house of Cotsford and Benson, after a flourishing career in Lancaster, finally removed to the wider sphere of London.

David and his Grace, lived to a good old age, saw their children grow up around them, and settle happily in life and in business, and while judiciously keeping the secret of their good fortune, they set apart every year, a considerable sum to be expended in works of Christian benevolence, as a thank-offering to Him whose providence had dealt so bountifully with them.

Thus, the gold intended to serve the ends of scheming politicians became a blessing to the poor in the narrow lanes of Lancaster and the crowded courts of London, and the story of the Cotsfords, however wonderful, does not stand alone, for an eminent banking firm in one of the midland counties is said to owe its origin to an incident exactly resembling that of the forgotten chest.

Source: *Religious Tract Society Book for the People,* 1893; but originally published much earlier at a date not yet established.

SECTION III - ESSAYS

1. Half-Way People

It is an old proverb, that 'extremes are dangerous.' Every village schoolboy can at least repeat, that all 'overlies are vice;' and from one generation to another men have commended the virtue of moderation. Doubtless all this is the language of experience; the world has had many warnings against ultras, written in strange characters and hard to be forgotten. History has prolonged, ages have renewed them, with much cost but little profit to the nations, and tradition has compressed their memories into those old saws and maxims that form the short-hand philosophy of the people. No marvel that the *via media,* was so earnestly recommended to the attention of mankind, by most of their numerous instructors, many an age since and before the Latin sages named it. If there be little to be learned or hoped for, it has also less peril and endurance than those far-leading paths that wind away through shine and shadow to goals which travellers little dream of on their entrance.

Many pass their days in this path of security, but few there be that find it for themselves; some are born to it; nature weighs the components of their character like a conscientious shopkeeper, determined to give neither too little nor too much, and turns them out of the scales nice weight for the world, and no more. They never do anything extraordinary, but live and die respectable people in their station, and are for the most part tolerably prosperous. Others are fenced in by their fortunes that rise like a wall on either hand to keep their doings moderate, till they learn to hope and wish and think, in moderation too.

There are some that choose the middle path for action, from a dread of the perils they might meet beyond in slippery places, to which their dreams go out continually, and they would follow them if they could but venture. These are men of untried plans and schemes, who give suggestions to more daring minds, but are never remarkable, and rarely satisfied. Fear is the ballast of such barks. A mighty comptroller, and one to which society owes both grudge and gratitude; but there are lives over which it exercises a more ungracious influence. In every age and land, among all ranks, how many varieties of character may there be found whose failures in the concerns of this world, and some that stretch into the next, are traceable to the cowardly habit of going only half-way. Farther on there is invariably a lion in one shape or other, some barrier they cannot pass, some step too wide for them to take, be it ever so requisite; and before that always paltry and often imaginary danger, their own interests, honour, or duty, and frequently the harvest of other lives, are abandoned.

Reader, if your stars have ever been so unfriendly as to connect you in any fashion with a character of this description, the pleasures of memory are not likely to consist in a recurrence to the subject; but hoping better things, it may be instructive to study the motions of half-way goers in general. Public and private history abounds with them, and they always cut a shabby figure, though appearance is their standing idol.

A half-way friend is the most brittle reed that ever humanity leaned on; other friendships may be broken by quarrels, estranged by absence, or weighed in the balance of adversity and found wanting, but his remains a perpetual deficiency. Give him your confidence and expect his in return, there will be something he won't believe, and something he will keep back, though ten chances to one but that point is necessary to the proper understanding of the whole; depend upon him for an obligation, and it may be forthcoming but at some difficulty, half-way in the business, his services will make a final pause, and neither persuasion nor necessity will ever induce them to advance farther. In danger or dispute, he takes just half your part, thereby at once embroiling himself, and giving advantage to the enemy. In defence of his friend he goes far enough for listeners to say, 'what efforts at whitewashing!' but suppresses the acquitting evidence, on account of some paltry self-committal which it might involve.

There is a ludicrous instance of this kind of friendship recorded of Sir Richard Steele, in *Tattler* and *Spectator* times. He had shown much friendship to the unhappy Savage, the poet, but after a variety of services and some duration of intimacy, it at length stuck fast, some say, on the point of introducing him to the Secretary of State, with whom

Steele was on friendly terms; others, on that of obliging him with a trifling loan; but certain it is, that the refusal so far exasperated that luckless poet – whose nature, partaking somewhat of his name, was still more vulgarized by the lower vices of civilisation – that he pursued him round and round his own apartment with a drawn sword; such weapons being assigned to gentlemen by the barbarism of the reigning fashion: and the consequences might have been tragical, had not the cries of Sir Richard, brought all within hearing to his rescue. The conduct of Charles the First towards the Earl of Strafford, is a fatal example of half-part-taking friendships. It is said to have caused the last regret of that ill-starred and worse guided monarch. Yet how many royal friends have acted exactly similar!

Among the trials consequent on the insurrection of Robert Emmet, in 1803, was that of a Dublin gentleman, the only witness against whom was a common informer, unfortunately corroborated by strong circumstantial evidence. His intimate friend, a Quaker merchant, appeared in his favour; but to the surprise of all who heard him, though evidently most anxious to do all in his power for the prisoner, his testimony was so wavering and defective, that the jury refused to credit it, and his friend was convicted. Many years after, when the near approach of death gave things, perhaps on both sides of the grave, a truer aspect, the merchant revealed a fact that had long hung on his conscience and memory, namely, that there were at the period of the trial letters in his possession, which, if read in court, must have exculpated the accused; but as they would have also unfolded his unsuccessful courtship of a lady, in the language of his sect, belonging to the vain world, neither his vanity nor his religious reputation would permit him to disclose them.

Let all ladies who have hearts to lose or break – and there are different opinions regarding their numbers – beware of half-way lovers. If there be no hindrance in the case, no obstacle to be surmounted, no years to wait or toil through; but funds, kindred, and the world's approbation all convenient, their affections may rise to the easy standard, and appear perfect after the fashion of untried things; but few courses are so clear, and any impediment is sufficient to bar their progress. Swains of this pattern never advance beyond their own ease, interest or vanity (in some one of the last mentioned they are always particularly strong,) and there lies their *ne plus ultra*. The moralist cannot mark their doings with the black band of vice; but justly considered, they are scarce less degrading in their selfish security, which pauses at no sacrifice but its own.

Swift could address some of his best verses, and most of his confidential letters, to Stella, whom he called the consolation of his life, when her days were numbered; but because the world considered that the admired dean should find a higher match, he offered up the woman's years piecemeal to its opinion, and the world pronounced a just verdict on his cringing vanity, by deserting his latter days, and stigmatizing his memory. Well was the censure merited! Poems and French letters about love and destiny were written to Vanessa also, but never an intimation of his private marriage with her rival, the public and gentlemanly acknowledgement of which would have saved his biography some sad and shameful pages; but that single step to the right was not taken, and the consequences, as well as the odes and epistles, remain on record, to make posterity regret that affection should have been so far misplaced and genius so miserably employed. There are and have been Swifts, possessed of neither the talents nor the celebrity that failed to make the Dean respectable, but never a whit less paltry in their doings. The world's bondsmen! the serfs of circumstances whose inclinations shrink from opposition, and tremble to miss advantage, without the resolution either to strive boldly with the one, or make barter with the other.

Lord Chesterfield's behaviour to Dr Johnson was a curious example of the half-way friend. The plan of Johnson's dictionary was presented to his lordship, and received with his wonted grace; but he quietly allowed the author to strive through seven years of labour and difficulties, till his work was on the eve of publication, and had been spoken of at court. Then the master of etiquette awoke, and published no less than two articles in *The World* – then at the head of periodical literature – filled with his and the age's compliments to the great lexicographer. 'After making great professions, he had for many years taken no notice of me; but when my dictionary was coming out, he fell a scribbling in *The World* about it,' was the characteristic observation of Johnson; and one passage he addressed to Lord Chesterfield on the subject is worthy to outlast all the nobleman's epistles of small advice. 'The notice which you have been pleased to take of my talents, had it been early, had been kind; but it has been delayed till I am indifferent, and cannot enjoy it; till I am solitary, and cannot impart it; till I am known, and do not want it.'

There are half-way enemies too – creatures who keep the grudge, and show it under every possible pretext; generally preferring times of calamity for that purpose, but never daring to come to open opposition, on account of something that might be said or lost. Such an enemy was the mother of Christian the Seventh of Denmark, to his unlucky queen, Matilda, when, after a long course of petty annoyance and surveillance of her daughter-in-law – neither the wisest nor most fortunate of ladies – she hurried to her son's chamber in tears, at the conclusion of a royal ball, and told him that it was his painful and imperative duty, for the honour of the Danish crown, to sign a warrant for the queen's immediate arrest. That warrant was put in force before the last of the festive lights were extinguished in the palace. Swords have hung by hairs, ay, and descended, in more kingly mansions than that of Dionysius.

Source: *The People's and Howitt's Journal, 1849.*

Title page of Chambers's Edinburgh Journal (1845)

2. A Chapter on Odd People

'Yes, sir,' said Dr Johnson once in reply to a remark of Boswell; 'every man who has brains is eccentric, because he sees and thinks for himself; and if he did not, minds would be all cut with compasses, and no rational man could endure society.' Doubtless the leviathan of literature, as both friends and enemies called him in his day, had learned, by means of his proverbial love of 'a good talk,' how much social life is enlivened by occasional obliquities of taste, and even of judgment.

'Defend me from pattern ladies and men of rule!' was the petition of a rather unruly poet, in which many who are not poets will be found to concur, for there seems a natural association between dullness and uniformity. Yet the widest deviations from received ideas, as regards external matters, are not always made by the ablest thinkers. All the world has heard, and probably by this time got tired of, the eccentricities of genius. They have been largely reported, and still more largely imitated, particularly those of the discreditable kind, since it was found out that great wit was allied to madness. Those who could never reach the former have adopted the latter as its nearest relation, forgetting that they were affecting only what disgraced their betters, and too frequently that which would have disgraced any grade of mind.

But the age for such affectations, even of the harmless order, is past; eccentricity is now known to be one of the liabilities, not the consequence of genius, and has been most prominently displayed in those who had no genius at all. These are smoothing-down days, and peculiarities appear above the surface, more rarely than they did in less polishing times; but uncelebrated oddities may still be encountered in every by-way and corner of life. The upland hamlet, the rural village, or the small country town, can generally boast a Miss or Mr Whimsy of its own, whose out-of-the-way sayings and doings will return among the pleasures of memory to some of its scattered denizens, in far-off scenes and years. Even in great cities, where the perpetual though changeful currents of business and society, are calculated to wear away the angularities of minds and manners, it is wonderful in what perfection they still exist.

The first Charles Mathews used to describe three meagre brothers, all men of business in New York, who always had their garments made double the fitting size, in order to save time and trouble in case their respective corporations should increase, an occurrence which seemed probable to them alone. The residents of another busy street in that same western city, about twenty years ago, may recollect an old man whose whim was still more remarkable. He was a bachelor with a decent income; and, strange to say, no miser, though he lived utterly alone, acted as his own attendant in his own department of housekeeping, and never admitted a single feminine assistant, as his special ambition was to be what he called independent of women. There were those who said the old boy had been slighted or aggrieved by some of the sex in his younger days: perhaps the story originated only in conjecture, but the advocates of woman's rights and mission would have been astonished at the legion of wrongs he could muster up when denouncing female tyranny, under which he affirmed the whole creation groaned. No misfortune, great or small, ever happened to any man within his knowledge which he could not trace, by a most elaborate process of reasoning, to some female hand. And one of his chief doctrines was that no man could admit one of the fair (by courtesy) within the walls of his domicile and escape absolute slavery. To preserve his own liberty, therefore, this original philosopher superseded the ladies in actual service, from stitching shirts to making tea. He is said to have acquired extraordinary proficiency, particularly in the former art, and always boasted to his friends that he was one independent man.

Lingerers in the state of celibacy are popularly believed to be more addicted to eccentricity than the wedded of mankind; on which belief a minutely ingenious philosopher once suggested the enquiry, 'Whether being single was the cause of their singularity or *vice versa*?' Certain it is that the special characteristics of the New York bachelor could exist in no other condition; yet it may be hoped that all the single are not singular, especially as some odd actors are occasionally found among the doubly-blessed.

I knew a married lady whose peculiar taste in dress formed the standing topic of conversation to the fairer portion of a country parish. She had been an heiress in a small way, and could therefore command some of the sinews of fashion; but she said no milliner should ever dictate to her, for she had an original fancy, and would not be put in uniform. This resolution she kept with the zeal of a patriot; never was the regimentalism of costume more defied than in the cut of her garments, while the boasted originality was displayed in an arrangement of colours, and an adaptation of materials, which set at naught all toilet regulations. Her favourite winter attire was a white flannel cloak lined with scarlet. She delighted in tartan boots; and when I last heard of her, she had just horrified the ladies of the neighbourhood by trimming her bonnet with broad-cloth.

Perhaps the most ordinary and unobtrusive form of eccentricity is favouritism with regard to certain articles. There was a man of rank some years ago in Paris, known to his acquaintance by the *soubriquet* of 'the shoe-gatherer,' from his habit of heaping up boots and shoes, new and old, till a large room in his residence was necessarily set apart for the purpose of containing them; and he was said rarely to have passed a shop of the kind without ordering home an additional supply.

A clergyman of my native village took a similar delight in wigs, and a hundred and fifty 'time defiers,' as a London wit designated those articles, were sold by auction on the good man's premises after his death. The rarest instance of this description I ever knew was that of a farmer whose enthusiasm rested on pots. He bought them, large and small, on every possible pretext, to the confusion of the kitchen-maid and the annoyance of his helpmate; till the latter, having a small taste of the Tartar in her composition, at length declared war against pot metal, and eventually won the day so far that, on her husband's occasional visits to the nearest market town, she was wont to shout after him the following adjuration, 'Mind, bring no pots home with you!' Her injunction was generally obeyed, for the lady might not be provoked with impunity. But when a supernumerary dram warmed the farmer's fancy, it would sometimes revert to the ancient channel, and he has been known to deposit a pot or two at a neighbouring cottage, as the dread of probable consequences occurred with the sight of his own chimney smoke.

Some persons are eccentric in their curiosity, and a troublesome kind of oddity it is at times to their neighbours, as they are apt to ask all manner of inconvenient questions. A family dispute, a lost situation, or a failure in business, is among their chosen subjects; and by way of securing authentic information, they make a point of applying to the parties most concerned. It was a genius of this order who, when Talleyrand was dismissed from office by the Emperor, sent him a long letter explicitly detailing all the reports in circulation against him, and concluding with a polite request to be informed which of them was true. A similar character on our own side of the British Channel one day mistaking Tyrone Power for a captain of his acquaintance who had just quitted the service under equivocal circumstances, seized the comedian by the button at Charing Cross, with, 'Oh, Captain Blake, I was sorry to hear it – 'pon my honour I was – but were you actually cashiered for cowardice?'

'I have not the honour to be Captain Blake, sir,' said Power, still led along by the button; 'and when you meet that gentleman, I advise you not to press the question.'

'Why,' said the blunt of brain, 'couldn't he tell me best?'

'Ah, yes, my dear fellow,' responded Power benevolently; 'but he might kick you!'

Probably the most eccentric expression of grief recorded is that of Madame du Deffand, of Walpole notoriety, who, being informed in the midst of a large party, that one of her intimate friends had died some hours before, ejaculated, '*Helas!* I shall not be able to take any supper!'

Eccentric prejudices are comparatively common; one occasionally meets with individuals who regard the use of animal food as the cause of all the ills that flesh is heir to; and a gentleman, formerly residing in Kent, put his confidence entirely in turnips as their universal remedy. Constitutional antipathies or affinities, unaccountable as they are in themselves, would perhaps account for these notions, as well as for those eccentric preferences of sights, sounds and odours, which are otherwise inexplicable. Persons have been known to dislike the smell of roses, and rather prefer that of garlic; others have relished the rasping of a file; the Dutch doctor, who saw nothing in all Paris to admire but the shambles, has doubtless brethren in many lands.

There are, however, peculiarities of taste which have their origin in the higher ground of our nature, and belong to minds of a finer fabric. Charles Lamb confessed that he admired a squint, because a girl to whom he had been attached in early life squinted prodigiously; and a lady of my acquaintance thought a club-foot interesting, from similar recollections. It is strange how seldom eccentricity takes an elevating or even an agreeable form; odd ways are rarely those of pleasantness, or peace either; though many of the world's notables have indulged in them, as stands recorded by better pens and ampler pages than mine. It is not always genius that makes one differ from his neighbours, but some heavy strength of character, considerable obstinacy, and at times right royal virtues, may be found among the oddfellows of creation.

One of the best-principled women I ever knew was possessed with the restless anxiety to learn not only the Christian names of every person she chanced to encounter, but those of all their relations in the ascending line. Her enquiries, which were vigorously pushed forward, in all companies, sometimes created most ludicrous annoyance to the parties interrogated, though I cannot recollect an instance of her getting beyond the great grandfather.

It has been observed that singular tastes and habits are less frequently found among the working-classes than in superior ranks; the pressing necessities of life generally requiring the utmost exertions of the former in continuous labour, leave them neither time nor means for indulging in peculiarities. There is no scope for eccentricity in such circumstances; yet where the bent is strong, it will make room for itself. Some years ago, a northern town of England, once famous in Border history, and now of some importance on one of our great railway lines, received an addition to its inhabitants, whose mode of conducting his pilgrimage through life, considering the path in which he journeyed, was something original. He was a man about thirty, tall, handsome, and of that sort of air generally known as genteel, on which point his singularity seemed to rest. The man avowed himself to be a native of London; his business was the sale and manufacture of muffins; and no one, so far as I heard, thought of enquiring after his name. He lived in a small cottage on the suburbs of the town, to which neither assistant, attendant nor visitor was known to have been admitted. There he made his muffins, and thence he issued to supply his customers as regularly as the English breakfast-hour came round.

But no London exquisite, prepared for a lounge in Bond Street or the Park, could appear with more fashionably-cut coat, faultless hat, or more stainless linen; from the polish of his boots to the whiteness of his gloves he was a perfect Brummel, always excepting the basket over his arm, which, however, was ingeniously contrived to resemble that usually carried by anglers. Out of that array he was never seen on the street. How it could be obtained or kept in order was a daily renewed wonder. People said there was a different dress worn at the cottage; and all the tailors of the town affirmed he made his own garments, as to the business of none had he given the smallest addition. His solitary leisure was spent in cleaning gloves, brushing up matters generally, and disciplining a couple of shirts; for that morning-sally was the joy of his life, and to be occasionally mistaken for a gentleman dandy, his only aim and reward.

This devoutly-wished-for consummation he attained at times, and one instance of it served to amuse the townspeople, to whose knowledge it came, for many a day. The daughter of a respectable merchant who had just returned from a London boarding-school, with a large importation of airs, and a profound admiration for everything showy and useless, chanced to meet the incomparable recluse on the first of her morning walks. The young lady came home overflowing with what she called the romantic circumstance of a distinguished young nobleman actually coming to rusticate in such a place on the pretext of angling in the celebrated salmon river. She knew he was Frederick Beauchamp, the brother of her particular friend Lady Theresa, daughter of the Earl of ---, who had introduced him to her just before leaving school. He had looked very much at her; she would bow to him on the next occasion.

True to her resolution, she sallied forth on the following day after an hour's extra dressing, and encountered the object of her solicitude on his usual morning rounds. Miss took the opportunity of saluting him in the crowded street before two elderly acquaintances, and her nod was most gravely returned.

'He cannot recollect me, I am so much grown!' said she, in a loud whisper.

'Do you know him?' enquired one of the ladies in company.

'Oh yes!' responded Miss. 'I met him frequently in London.'

'Indeed!' replied the querist; 'he has been here for two years, and they call him the Muffin-Man.'

Her neighbours averred that, after that revelation, the particular friend of Lady Theresa was never in a hurry to recognise distinguished-looking strangers; but with the eccentric muffin-man I close my recollections of oddities.

Source: *Chambers's Edinburgh Journal, 1849*

3. The Philosophy of Would Be

It is long since this world was called busy. Writers of every age have said so of their own generation, as they toiled and fretted with it till the dust. Doubtless their words were true. Mankind always have been as they still are, careful and troubled about many things. Providing for present wants, or laying up for future projects, seems sufficient to keep the great mass in full occupation; yet how often are their recognised pursuits and conditions chequered with a restless striving after aims far distant and dissimilar, which never multiplies the gain, but always increases the trouble.

I am not what I would be, is the language of many lives; not in the higher moral sense, though it is to be hoped that some do intend being better and wiser than they actually appear; but in what class or locality may not one meet with people anxious to be mistaken (if it were but temporarily) for something they are not; and who intermingle at times, whimsically enough, with their own widely different avocations, some gathered leaven of the position or business which engrosses their mental regards?

Scott's character of the law-loving Saddlletree, who enacted the jurisconsult while he mended harness, is not only a case in point, but one with many parallels. I once knew a schoolmaster in a rural parish, a laborious teacher and most pacific man, who had never looked on war in all the days of his existence, and who enjoyed a local celebrity for classical learning and mathematical knowledge; but these honours appeared poor and contemptible in his private judgment, compared with the glory and gratification of being taken for a military officer. To this end a considerable portion of his spare time –and the article was meted out to him in scanty measure – was spent in the acquisition of regimental airs and phrases, which were occasionally displayed to the amusement of his country neighbours; and so much at home with all the battles and sieges of the Peninsula did the good man become in the course of studious years, that strangers who heard him for the first time were in the habit of enquiring in what regiment he had served. Nor was it with the smallest diminution of ardour that he declared his actual profession, and the revelation was regularly followed by another that he was born with a military genius; but one mistake of the kind was sufficient to secure his goodwill for life.

By a similar assumption, men far removed from the ordinary rank of rulers take upon themselves, as it were, privately, the burden of state affairs. There is scarcely a small burgh or country town that does not number among its inhabitants some amateur statesman, to whom every movement in foreign policy and every change in the cabinet is a more engrossing subject of consideration that anything connected with the trade or toil to which his external life is devoted. It is curious, too, that the most complete and earnest politicians of this order are generally found in such quiet corners rather than amid the stirring interests and quick-coming news of cities, and that their ostensible occupations should be almost invariably of the sedentary kind. Is it owing to what old philosophers have called the perpetual contradiction of mind and matter, that outward limitations so evidently contribute to mental activity and enable the imaginations to grasp great things, till the worker on bench or loom becomes the associate of opposition M.P.'s or the colleague of cabinet ministers, without the one's risk or the other's responsibility? Medical authorities have also remarked that cases of insanity, or fanaticism, which approaches it, are most abundant in those trades. Out of how many wells by the wayside of life can there be 'drawn both sweet water and bitter?'

It may be owing to the almost boundless influence and the widespread though profitless honours in all times attending the profession of literature, that its mere seeming has been the life-aim and endeavour of many who apparently possessed enough besides. What a world of small pains, how much of misapplied energy, anxiety, and envy, has it cost many an owner of estates and titles to make the public sensible of his claim on authorship! What poems, what novels, have thus been published at the request of admiring friends, or in aid of some charitable institution! With what tours in France and travels in Italy have the trade and the trunkmaker alike been over accommodated! It is for the honour and safety of literature, that in no pursuit is distinction more difficult of acquisition without real merit, and in none can the aids of extraneous circumstances so little avail. The luckless actor's demand, 'a clear stage and no favour,' is not indeed always the rule, even in the republic of letters. The influence of position or connections operates at times to raise a shout for genius which does not exist; but such artificial triumphs are temporary, and rarely outlast the first examination.

Theodore Hook used to tell a story of a nobleman whose gift was not the pen, but once in his youth he wrote (no matter how) a tragedy. It was the grand achievement of his life, and had come out with a flourish of trumpets that had captivated the fashionables of London, till another novelty succeeded and his lordship's tragedy was forgotten. He lived on the glory of that fortnight till extreme old age. He held office in the cabinet, travelled much, and of course met many strangers; but for each and all of them, whether young or old, sage or simple, the determined author had but one question, which was always asked on the earliest opportunity, 'Tell me, upon your honour, have you ever heard of my tragedy?' Woe to those that answered in the negative. On them was immediately inflicted a full account of its plot, composition and success; concluding with an earnest admonition to order the work directly from the nearest bookseller.

No position is too elevated for this form of the would-be principle to find an entrance. It has appeared in full operation even at the height of thrones; and those whose very station ensured them the deference, and, what is often as much valued, the notice of the world, have striven strangely, to affect that unannexed distinction. Frederick II of Prussia, in the midst of his military triumphs and successful statesmanship (an almost absolute monarch in the days when royalty was questioned by neither press nor people,) was not content with being known only as a great king, but expended both time and temper in a vain effort to pass also with his age for a luminary of the then fashionable French school, attempting by turns the poet and the philosopher.

In spite of the proverbial assistance which flattery lends to kingly productions, Frederick's French letters and some other fragments, still remaining as they came from the royal hand, bear witness to a want of grammatical knowledge, and even orthography, which would amuse a modern school girl. In short, his early education was defective; the great king made but a small author; and on the occasion of their famous quarrel, Voltaire published to the world (and it sometimes believed him) that the only thing original in his majesty's compositions was the bad grammar, which he had corrected.

The literary ambition of men in high place has played sad vagaries in times when power was less restrained and interrogated than it is in our own generation. Henry VIII was possessed by this in addition to many worse spirits; and as, after the fashion of his times, he sought distinction through the medium of theology, it made him a grievous meddler with other men's consciences. When James I wrote his book against witchcraft, and sent a copy to every prince in Europe, a wit of the age remarked that each sovereign in turn said something complimentary regarding it, but not one that he had read the work. Its theme was that of the multitude, yet who can doubt that the monarch's endeavours after literary celebrity were promoting causes of that disgraceful persecution on which no enlightened mind can look back without special shame and sorrow for the species? Witch-finding was patronised by royal authorship, and the impulse thus given to the popular delusion of that age alone accounts for its terrible pre-eminence in Britain and her colonies.

What bitter fruits even tuneful aspirations may produce when grafted on arbitrary power, was long ago experienced by two Persian poets, whose different lines of conduct under the circumstances have been the subject of much remark and some controversy among the critics of their country. One of the shahs having determined to signalise himself above ordinary kings, once wrote a poem, and summoned the most notable bard in his dominions to hear and give his opinion of the composition. The shah read his own production; and the poet, after sundry exhortations to candour, proceeded to criticise; but his opinion differed so far from that of his royal composer, that, before the review was half finished, he was dubbed an ass, and commanded to be confined in the stable among those useful quadrupeds. His sojourn there was not long; the shah, supposing there might have been some truth in his observations, set about improving his poem for the benefit of posterity; and, as soon as the changes were effected, he summoned the poet once more, and admonished him to give a just verdict; but scarce had the first revision been read when the impracticable bard exclaimed, 'Eldest son of the Prophet, send me back to the stable!' On this, the shah at once dismissed him and, by way of a more memorable lesson, summoned his less popular rival (for literary fends and jealousies have existed in Persia as well as in England). Warned by the fortunes of the first critic, the second listened to the shah's poem with breathless attention; then requested a sight of the manuscript, and time to form his judgment upon it; hinting the chief beauties lay far beneath the surface, and his own mind was distracted by many cares of the financial order. The shah commended his penetration, presented him with a purse of gold to relieve the pressure of present necessity (observing there was more in the royal treasury), and reminded him that he would accept nothing but conscientious criticism. The poet hurried to his house, packed up his moveables immediately, burned the shah's manuscript, and started for the Christian frontier; but even the flights of poet's sometimes terminate abruptly. The shah's officers were soon on his track, they caught him within a league of the Euphrates, and he was marched back into the royal presence. 'Wretch,' cried the infuriated shah, 'Where is our magnificent poem, and why hast thou fled?'

'I confess my fault,' said the poet, depositing himself in oriental fashion at the foot of the throne; 'the inestimable manuscript is destroyed. I burned it in the desperation of my envy, and afterwards fled to escape merited punishment! Oh son of the Prophet, remember that a poet has nothing but his fame, and who could endure to be eclipsed for ever!' The chronicle relates that the bard on this confession, received a rather lengthy lecture against the sin of envy, but he was pardoned and subsequently became the favourite poet of the shah; who, by his recommendation, commenced a still longer poem, and would have finished it, if his vizier had not assassinated him and usurped the kingdom.

How lucky that all the world of would-bes are not kings, as kings were once, before the nations practically knew them to be but men! The conduct just described was more natural for a shah than one would on first sight imagine. But however widely men may be separated by the casualties of rank or the variety of their endowments, there is still a family resemblance in their follies; for each, according to time and opportunity, endeavours to exact some amount of homage from his favourite assumption.

One of Pope's letters supplies an amusing instance of this description, in his acquaintance with the celebrated Lord Halifax. Above his well-won reputation as an able statesman, a brilliant wit, and an accomplished orator, his lordship was ambitious of a critical taste in poetry. When Pope was preparing his Homer for publication, Halifax was one of his patrons, and the first three books were read at his house, one evening, in the presence of Addison, Congreve and Garth. Their host seemed deeply interested, but at several passages interrupted the poet with – 'I beg your pardon, Mr Pope, but there is something in that passage that does not quite please me. Be so good as to mark the place, and consider it a little at your leisure. I am sure you can give it a better turn.' Pope did consider the passages at his leisure, but could not discover how to please his lordship; and the criticism of a patron was not to be overvalued in those days. At length his friend Garth, who seems to have been initiated in such mysteries, advised him to let the verses remain as they were, and call on Lord Halifax in three months; thank him for his kind observations and read them to him as amended. 'I followed his advice.' says the not over scrupulous poet, 'waited on Lord Halifax some time after, said I hoped he would find his objections to those passages removed, read them to him exactly as they were at first; when his lordship exclaimed, Ay, now they are perfectly right, nothing can be better.'

It is a strange propensity of human pride to grasp at something more with hands already too full. Every man has his gift, says the proverb, and some have many; but how few are satisfied to shine only through their own approved talents. Hence those who have achieved applause and excellence in one department, frequently exhibit nothing but deficiency in aiming at another. The clever novelist may be but a poor historian, and the most successful dramatist rarely produces a popular romance; while the failure of the best authors in all their attempts at commerce is notorious. On every side there is a bound set to human abilities which they cannot pass. Though spoken at different points, the injunction of nature to each and all is, - 'Hitherto shalt thou come, and no farther.' Some, indeed, possess a variety of talents; and instances are not wanting of individuals who have excelled almost equally in different pursuits. Shakespeare is said to have done his own dramas justice on the stage; and Burke was admired as an author, an orator, and a politician. But there are also certain gifts which appear to be incompatible, and are never found united. History has no record of one who was great in poetry and mechanics, and no famous mathematician has ever shone as an orator.

Few minds know, like Samson, wherein their own strength lies. Many aim at what they would, rather than what they can be; and a similar error on the part of relatives and guardians occasions those mistakes in the selection of professions which often prove so disastrous in the after course of life. Many a shabby barrister might have kept a respectable warehouse; and there are unlucky divines who could have farmed to some purpose. On the contrary, the would-bes of ordinary life always aspire; some station more prominent than that which they naturally occupy, some pursuit which society regards as more distinguished, or at least more notable, is the aim of their fancy and the object of their regret for having missed; on which particular they usually keep a fund of accusations against their families, their stars, and the world collectively, in continual readiness. This habit of mind almost invariably leads the young to imitate the airs or eccentricities of the admired profession; which, by the way, are considerably exaggerated in their practice. Some aspirants follow a living and some an imaginary model; but all neglect or undervalue the duties of that vocation, by which, in common parlance, they live. The latter procedure, indeed, forever distinguishes the mere pretext of pride from the bent of real genius. Captain Cook was a wool-comber's apprentice, and Gifford a cobbler's boy. The one studied navigation in his leisure hours, and the other wrote sentences with an awl on scraps of old leather; but both were esteemed useful and industrious youths by their respective masters.

Many lives consist of a continual offering up of what the individual is to that which he would be, though the last estate exceeds the first in nothing but the man's imagination and the greater sacrifices it demands. Under that delusion the families of honest tradesmen struggle to become fashionables, and respectable merchants imitate the follies of nobility. Nay, the votaries of the press themselves are not free from it. The builder of Abbotsford exhausted his powers in vain to found an aristocratic family; and many a popular author besides has lavished his resources and done despite to literature in a fruitless endeavour to emulate the habits of rank and fashion. Oh, the poverty of human pride, that could descend to such small eminences, when it might occupy so much higher ground! It reminds one of Commodus laying aside the imperial purple to contend with gladiators for the applause of the amphitheatre. There are those whose existence is worn away between conflicting aims which nature or the state of things has made irreconcilable. They are the servants of two masters at mortal feud, but will give up neither, and therefore serve each but indifferently, and themselves not at all. Many and strange are the abuses of would-be-ism (if one may coin a new substantive); but whence is its origin? Is it from the universal want of something beyond the realities of our present existence, that deficiency which Frederick the Great found in his throne, and my country schoolmaster in his realm of juveniles? Is it because the practical experience of every condition and pursuit returns such sad accounts of loss and dissatisfaction, that the mind learns to dramatise, as it were, our outward state, by assuming the character and costume of another? Nor does resemblance to the theatricals end here. How many of those aimers at other people's gifts and glories would willingly change place, possessions, and personality, to be 'the very envied creature,' any more than the actor would desire to become in serious earnest the tragic hero he represents for the evening. The Persian shah would scarcely have wished to be the poet he sent to the stable; and many a political tradesman would tire of being prime minister, especially in times like the present. It is the good things of different estates that men strive to unite, because the portion assigned to each is small; and as old romances are wont to relate their hero's adventures and success unalloyed by the wear and tear, the weariness, ay, and the meanesses of actual life, attending alike on its labours and its gains, so life's great gilder, the imagination, at once presents her would-be with the crown, but spares him all the crosses of the reality.

There was a Greek bishop once, who affirmed it had been revealed to him in a dream that in the world to come every individual would be the very counterpart of all he had desired to be in this. He added that such was the means of future reward and punishment; but his orthodoxy being questioned by the Patriarch of Constantinople, the good bishop explained matters in the following fashion: 'Excellent father, when I was a child, and played beside the Eurotus, I saw my young companions imitate the state and grandeur of the old grown world, and walk as kings and emperors with sceptres of reeds and crowns of rushes; now I behold most men of my generation intent on playing even with themselves as spectators some part which is not their own; wherefore it seems to me that our souls are yet in their childhood, and these poor and ill-aimed efforts foreshadow (but truly I know not how) the more ample state to which they are destined; and this is all that was taught me in my dream.'

Source: *Hogg's Instructor,* 1849.

4. Letters

Neither history nor tradition tells us aught of the first letter – who was its writer, and on what occasion; how it was transmitted or in what manner answered. The Chinese, the Hindoo, and the Scandinavian mythologies have each tales regarding the inventors of writing, and the rest of those that by pre-eminence may be called human arts; but concerning the beginner of mankind's epistolary correspondence, neither they nor the classic poets- who, by the way, volunteered many an ingenious story on subjects far less important – have given us the least account.

Pope says –

"Heaven first taught letters for some wretch's aid -
Some banished lover, or some captive maid."

The poet evidently refers to the letter-writing art, and it may be so, for aught we can tell; but with all submission to his superior knowledge, banished lovers and captive maids have rarely been the transmitters of such useful inventions. Certainly, whoever first commenced letter-writing, the world has long been his debtor. It is long since the Samaritans wrote a letter against the builders of Jerusalem to Artaxerxes, and it may be observed that the said letter is the earliest epistle mentioned in any history. Older communications appear to have been always verbal, by means of heralds and messengers. Homer, in his account of all the news received and sent between the Greeks and Trojans, never refers to a single letter. The scribe's occupation was not altogether unknown in those days, but it must have been brought to considerable perfection before efforts in the epistolary style were made. That ancient language of picture and symbol, in which Egypt expressed her wisdom, was undoubtedly the earliest mode of writing; but however calculated to preserve the memory of great historical events amid the daily life, and toil, and changes of nations, it was but poorly fitted for the purpose of correspondence. How could compliments or insinuations be conveyed by such an autograph? Letters must have been brief and scanty in the hieroglyphic times; yet doubtless not without some representations, for the unalphabeted have combined to hold mutual intelligence by many a sign or emblem, especially in those affairs designated of the heart, as they above all others contribute to ingenuity. Hence came the Eastern language of flowers, which with Oriental literature and mythology, is now partially known over the civilised world. In its native clime this natural alphabet is said to be so distinctly understood, that the most minute intimations are expressed by it; but the more frank and practical courtship of Europe has always preferred the pen as the channel of communication, which, besides, its greater power of enlargement, prevents those mistakes into which the imperfectly-initiated are apt to fall with flowers. For instance, there is a story of a British officer in Andalusia, who, having made a deep impression on the heart of a certain alcaide's daughter, in one of the small towns of that half-Moorish province, and receiving from her one morning a bouquet, the significance of which was – 'My mother is in the way now, but come to visit me in the twilight,' supposed in his ignorance, and perhaps presumption, that he was invited to an immediate appointment: whereupon he hurried to the house, just in time to meet the venerable signora, when the lady of his heart boxed his ears with her own fair hands, and vowed she would never again send flowers to a stupid Englishman.

In fine contrast to this sample of misunderstanding stands forth the dexterity with which an Irish serving-maid contrived to signify, by symbols of her own invention, her pleasure on a still more trying occasion. Kitty, though a belle in her class, could neither read nor write; but her mistress's grown-up daughter undertook, as a labour of love, to carry on a correspondence between her and a certain hedge schoolmaster in the neighbourhood, who laid siege to Kitty's heart and hand on account of a small deposit in the savings' bank, and that proverbial attraction which learned men are said to find in illiterate ladies. The schoolmaster was, however, providently inclined to fixing on the mind of his future partner an impression of his own superiority sufficient to outlast the wear and tear of married life, and therefore wooed chiefly by long and learned letters, to which Kitty responded in her best style, leaving to her volunteer secretary what she called 'the grammar' of her replies; besides declaring, with many hardly-complimentary observations on the schoolmaster's person and manners, that she had not the slightest interest in the affair, but only, in her own words, 'to keep up the craythur's heart.' Thus the courtship had proceeded prosperously through all the usual stages, when at length the question, *par excellence*, was popped (of course on paper). Kitty heard that epistle read with wonted disdain, but alas for human confidence! There was something in her answer with which she could not trust the writer of so many; for, after all her scorn, Kitty intended to say 'Yes,' and her mode of doing so merits commemoration. In solitude that evening, beside the kitchen hearth, she sketched on a sheet of white paper, with the help of a burned stick, a rude representation of a human eye, and enclosing a small quantity of wool, despatched it next morning to the impatient swain by the hand of his head scholar – those primitive tokens expressing to Kitty's mind the important words, 'I will,' which the teacher, strange to say, understood in the same sense, and their wedding took place, to the unqualified amazement of Kitty's amanuensis.

Epistolary forms and fashions have had their mutations like all other human things. The old Eastern mode of securing letters was by folding them in the shape of a roll, and winding round them a thin cord, generally of silk, as the luxury of letters was known only to the rich. In the case of billets-doux – for Eastern lovers did not always speak by flowers when the pen was at their command, enthusiastic ladies sometimes substituted those long silken strings which, from time immemorial, Oriental women have worn in their hair – a proceeding which was understood to indicate the deepest shade of devotedness.

The mythic importance attached to these hair strings must indeed have been great, as history records that a certain prince, whose dominions were threatened by Mithridates, the great king of Pontus – like other great men, a troublesome neighbour in his day – sent the latter a submissive epistle, offering homage and tribute, and bound with the hair-strings of his nineteen wives, to signify that he and his were entirely at the monarch's service. The custom of securing letters by cords came through the Greek empire into Europe in the middle ages; but the use of the seal seems still earlier, as it is mentioned in Old Testament history. Ancient writers speak of it as an Egyptian invention, together with the signet ring, so indispensable throughout the classic world, and regarded as the special appendage of sovereignty in the feudal times.

Of all the letters the Egyptians wrote on their papyrus, no specimens now remain, except perhaps those scrolls in the hands of mummies, referred to by early Christian authors as epistles sent to deceased friends by those unreturning messengers; and they it may be presumed, were at the best but formal letters, since no reply was ever expected. The classic formula for correspondence, 'Augustus to Julius, greeting.' is now preserved only in letters-patent, or similar documents. That brief and unvarying style has long been superseded in every language of Europe by a graduated series of endearing terms, rising with the temperature of attachment from 'Dear Sir,' or 'Madam,' to a limit scarcely assignable, but it lies somewhere near 'Adored Thomas,' or 'Margery.'

Masters of the fine arts as they were, those ancient nations came far short of moderns in that of letter-writing. The few specimens of their correspondence that have reached us are either on matters of public business, or dry and dignified epistles from one great man to another, with little life and less gossip in them. It is probable that their practice was somewhat limited, as the facilities of the post-office were unknown to Greece and Rome – the entire agency of modern communication being to the classic world represented only by the post of courier, who formed part of the retinue of every wealthy family. The method of writing in the third person, so suitable for heavy business or ceremony, is evidently a classical bequest. It does not appear to have been practised in England till about the beginning of the eighteenth century, though it was early in use among the continental nations. Louis XIV used to say it was the only style in which a prince should permit himself to write; and in the Far East, where it had been in still older repute, the Chinese informed his missionaries that ever since they had been taught manners by the Emperor Tae Sing, no inferior would presume to address a man of rank in any other form, especially as a law of the said emperor had appointed twenty blows of the bamboo for that infraction of plebeian duty.

Of all human writings, letters have been preserved in the smallest proportion. How few of those which the best-informed actors in great events or revolutions must have written, have been copied by elder historians or biographers! Such documents are, by their nature, at once the least accessible and the most liable to destruction; private interests, feelings, and fears, keep watch against their publication; but even when these were taken out of the way, it is to be feared that the narrow-minded habit of overlooking all their wisdom deemed minute, which has made the chronicles of nations so scanty, and many a life in two volumes such dull reading, also induced learned compilers to neglect, as beneath their search, the old letters bundled up in dusty chest or corner, till they served a succeeding generation for waste paper. Such mistakes have occasioned heavy losses to literature. Time leaves no witnesses in the matter of history and character equal to these. How many a disputed tale, on which party controversy has raged, and laborious volumes have been written, would the preservation of one authentic note have set at rest for ever?

The practical learning of our times, in its search after confirmation and detail, amply recognises the importance of old letters; and good service has been done to both history and moral philosophy, by those who have given them to the press from state-paper office and family bureau. In such collections one sees the world's talked- of -and- storied people as they were in private business, in social relations, and in what might be justly designated the status of their souls. In spite of the proverbial truism that paper never refuses ink, and falsehood can be written as well as spoken, the correspondence of every man contains an actual portrait of the writer's mind, visible through a thousand disguises, and bearing the same relation to the inward man that a correct picture bears to the living face; without change or motion, indeed, but telling the beholder of both, and indicating what direction they are likely to take.

The sayings of wits and the doings of oddities long survive them in the memory of their generation – the actions of public men live in history, and the genius of authors in their works; but in every case the individual, him or herself, lives in letters. One who carried this idea still further, once called letter-writing the Daguerreotypes of mind – ever leaving on paper its true likeness, according to the light in which it stands for the time; and he added, like the sun's painting, apt to be most correct in the less pleasant lines and lineaments. Unluckily, this mental portraiture, after the fashion of other matters, seems less perceptible to the most interested parties. Many an unconcerned reader can at this day trace in Swift's epistles the self-care and worship which neither Stella nor Vanessa could have seen without a change in their histories.

Cardinal Mazarin, however, used to say that an ordinary gentleman might deceive in a series of interviews, but only a complete tactician in one of letters; 'that is,' observed his eminence, 'if people don't deceive themselves.' The cardinal's statement strikingly recalls, if it does not explain, a contemporary remark that the most successful courtships, in the fullest sense of that word, were carried on with the help of secret proxies in the corresponding department. The Count de Lauson, whose days, even to a good old age, were equally divided between the Bastille and the above-mentioned pursuit, in which he must have been rather at home – for though a poor gentleman with little pretensions to family, still less to fortune, and no talents that the world gave him credit for, he contrived in his youth to marry a princess of the blood-royal of France, who had refused half the kings of Europe, and been an Amazon in the war of the Fronde; and in his age a wealthy court belle – this Count de Lauson declared that he could never have succeeded in his endeavours after high matches but for a certain professional letter-writer of Versailles, on whose death he is said to have poured forth unfeigned lamentations in the presence of his last lady.

Letters always appear to have been peculiarly powerful in the count's country. Madame de Genlis, whose 'Tales of the Castle' and 'Knights of the Swan' delighted at least the juveniles of a now-departing generation, was believed to have made a complete conquest, even before first sight, of the nobleman whose name she bears, by a single letter, sent to a lady at whose house he was an admiring visitor, when she unadvisedly showed him the epistle. An anxiously-sought introduction and a speedy marriage followed; but the scandal-mongers of the period averred that their separation, which took place some years after was owing among other circumstances, to an anonymous letter received by the baron himself.

Frederick the Great used to call the French the first letter-writers of Europe, and it is probable that their national turn for clever gossip

Richmond-upon-Thames: Frances lived there between 1866 and 1879.

gives to their epistles a sort of general interest, for in no other country have letters formed so large a portion of published literature. This was particularly true in Frederick's own age. Never did a death or a quarrel take place – and the latter was not rare among the *savants* of that period – but comfort or satisfaction was sought in the immediate publication of every scrap of correspondence, to the manifold increase of disputes and heart-burnings. Some of the most amusing volumes extant were thus given to the world; and Madame Dunoyer's, though scarcely of that description, must not be forgotten from the tale of its origin. When Voltaire was a young attaché to the French embassy at the Hague, with no reputation but that of being unmanageable by his family and confessor, he was on billet-doux terms, it seems, with madame's daughter; but madame found that he was poor, or something like it, for in no other respect was the lady scrupulous. Her veto was therefore laid on the correspondence, which nevertheless survived under interdict for some time, till Voltaire left the embassy, and it died of itself; for he wrote '*Oedipe*,' became talked of by all Paris, and noticed by the Marquis de Vellars. Gradually the man grew great in the eyes of his generation, his fame as a poet and philosopher filled all Europe, not forgetting the Hague; and when it had reached the zenith, Madame Dunoyer collected his letters to her daughter, which remained in her custody, the receiver being by this time married, and published them at her own expense in a handsomely-bound volume. Whether to be revenged on fortune for permitting her to miss so notable a son-in-law, or on him for obeying her commands, it is now impossible to determine, but her book served to show the world that the early billet-doux of a great genius might be just as milk-and-watery as those of common people.

Indeed, letter publishing seems to have been quite the rage in the eighteenth century. The Secretary La Beaumelle stole all Madame de Maintenon's letters to her brother, setting forth her difficulties in humouring Louis XIV, and printed them at Copenhagen. Some copies were obligingly forwarded to Versailles, but madame assured the king they were beneath his royal notice, which, being confirmed by his confessor, was of course believed; but the transaction looks like retributive justice on her well-known practice of keeping sundry post-office clerks in pay to furnish a copy of every letter sent or received by the principal persons at court, not excepting even the royal family. Among these were copied the celebrated letters of the Dauphiness Charlotte Elizabeth of Bavaria, which now, in good plain print, present to all readers of taste in that department a complete chronicle of all the scandal, gossip, and follies of Versailles; and that princess, whose pride stood so high on her family quarterings, was gravely rebuked, and obliged to ask pardon seven years after for certain uncomplimentary passages in her epistles regarding them when she first came to court as nursery governess to the king's children.

Dangerous approvers have old letters been from throne to cottage. Many a specious statement, many a fair profession, ay, and many a promising friendship, have they shaken down. Readers, have a care of your deposits in the post-office; they are pledges given to time. It is strange, though true, how few historical characters are benefited by the publication of their letters, surviving, as such things do, contemporary interests and prejudices, as well as personal influence.

There must be something of the salt that will not lose its savour there to make them serve the writers in the eyes of posterity. What strange confidence the age of hoop and periwig put in letter-writing! Divines published their volumes of controversy or pious exhortation, made up of epistles to imaginary friends. Mrs Chapone's letters to her niece nourished the wisdom of British belles; while Lord Chesterfield's to his son were the glass of fashion for their brothers; and Madame de Sevigne's to her daughter, written expressly for publication, afforded models for the wit, elegance, and sentiment of every circle wherein her language was spoken. The epistolary style's inherent power of characterisation naturally recommended it to the construction of their novels, and many a tale of fame and fashion in its day, besides 'La Nouvelle Heloise,' and 'Sir Charles Grandison,' was ingeniously composed of presumed correspondence.

Chinese literature is said to possess numerous fictions in that form; but it is not to be regretted that modern novelists, whose name is more than legion, pass it by in favour of direct narrative; for, under the best arrangement, a number of letters can give it but a series of views, telling the principal's tale in a broken, sketch fashion, and leaving little room for the fortunes of second-rate people, who are not always the lowest company in a novel. Tours and travels tell pleasantly in letters, supposing of course the letters to be well written; for some minds have such a wondrous affinity for the commonplace, that the most important event or exciting scene sinks to the every-day level under their pen.

Sir Andrew Mitchell, who was British ambassador to Prussia during the seven years' war, writes from the camp before Prague concerning that great battle which turned the scale of power in Germany, and served Europe to talk of till the French Revolution, in a style, but for the quotations from the bulletin, suitable to the election of some civic alderman; and a less known traveller, writing to a friend of the glare of Moscow's burning, which he saw from a Russian country house, reddening the northern night, describes it as 'a very impressive circumstance, calculated to make one guard against fire.'

It has been calculated that, as a general rule, poets write the best and schoolmasters the worst letters. That the former, in company with literary men of any order, should be at least interesting correspondents seems probable; but why the instructors of youth should be generally stricken with deficiency in letter-writing is not so easy of explanation.

Some one has also observed that, independent of mental gifts and graces, characters somewhat cold and frivolous generally write the most finished letters, and instanced Horace Walpole, whose published epistles even in our distant day commanded a degree of attention never to be claimed by those of his superior contemporaries – the highly-gifted Burke and the profound Johnson. It may be that the court gossip in and upon which Horace lived has done much for the letters from Strawberry Hill, but the vein must have been there; and the abilities that shine in the world of action or of letters, the conversational talents or worthiness of soul, do not make the cleverest correspondent.

Count Stadion, prime minister to the elector of Mayence, according to Goethe, hit on an easy method of making an impression by letters. He obliged his secretary, Laroche, to practise his handwriting, which it appears he did with considerable success; and says the poet in his own memoirs, being 'passionately attached to a lady of rank and talent, if he stopped in her society to late at night, his secretary was in the meantime sitting at home, and hammering out the most ardent love-letters; the count chose one of these, and sent it that very night to his beloved, who was thus necessarily convinced of the inextinguishable fire of her passionate adorer.'

'Helas!' as Madame d'Epigny remarked when turning over the printed epistles of a deceased friend, 'one can never guess how little truth the post brings one;' but from the following tradition, it would seem the less the better. Among the old-world stories of Germany are many regarding a fairy chief or king, known from rustic times as Number Nip, or Count-the-Turnips. One of his pranks was played in an ancient inn of Heidelberg, where, on a December night, he mixed the wine with a certain essence distilled from the flowers of Elfland, which had the effect of making all who tasted it tell nothing but truth with either tongue or pen till morning. The series of quarrels which took place in consequence round the kitchen fire belong not to the present subject; but in the red parlour there sat, all from Vienna, a poet, a student, a merchant, and a priest. After supper, each of these remembered that he had a letter to write – the poet to his mistress, the merchant to his wife, the priest to the bishop of his diocese, and the student to his bachelor uncle, Herr

Weisser of Leopoldstadt, who had long declared him his heir. Somehow next morning they were all at the post-office beseeching their letters back; but the mail had been despatched, and the tale records how, after that evening's correspondence, the poet's liege lady dismissed him, the merchant and his wife were divorced, the priest never obtained preferment, and none of the letters were answered except the student's, whom Herr Weisser complimented on having turned out such a prudent, sensible young man, but hoped he wouldn't feel disappointed as himself intended to marry immediately.

The most curiously-characteristic letters now made public property are those of Sir Walter Raleigh to Queen Elizabeth, written from the Tower (to which the historian of the world was committed for a wedding without her majesty's permission), and in the highest tone of desperation that a banished lover could assume; the correspondence between Frederick of Prussian and Voltaire, then of France, after what was called their reconciliation, beginning with the grandest compliments, and ending with reminiscences of quite another kind, particularly that from the royal pen, which opens with, 'You who from the heights of philosophy look down on the weakness and follies of mankind,' and concludes with the charge of appropriating candle-ends; and the epistles of Rousseau during his residence in England, which alternate between discoveries of black conspiracies against his life and fame, and threats of adjournment to the workhouse, if his friends would not assist him to live in a better style than most country gentlemen of the period.

There are printed samples with whose writers fame has been busy; but who can say what curiosities of writing daily mingle with the mass that pours through the London Post-Office? Can it be this continual custody and superintendence of so large a share of their fellow-creatures' wisdom, fortunes, and folly, that endows post-office functionaries in every quarter with such an amount of proverbial crustiness, if the word be admissible?

Do they, from the nature of their business, know too much about the public to think them worth civility, so that nobody has yet discovered a very polite postmaster or man? A strange life the latter leads in our great cities. The truest representative of destiny seems his scarlet coat, seen far through street and lane; at one door he leaves them news of failure and ruin, and at another the intelligence of a legacy. Here his message is the death of a friend, while to the next neighbour he brings tidings of one long absent, or the increase of kindred; but without care or knowledge of their import, he leaves his letters at house after house, and goes his way like a servant of time and fortune, as he is, to return again, it may be, with far different news, as their tireless wheels move on. Are there any that have never watched for his coming? The dwellers in palaces and garrets, large families, and solitary lodgers, alike look out for him with anxious hope or fear. Strange it is for one to read over those letters so watched and waited for when years have passed over since their date, and the days of the business, the friendship, or perhaps the wooing, to which they belong are numbered and finished!

How has the world without and within been altered to the correspondents since they were written? Has success or ill fortune attended the speculations by which they set such store? What have been their effects on outward circumstances and through that certain channel on the men? Has the love been forgotten? Have the friends become strange, or enemies? Have some of them passed to the land whose inhabitants send back no letters? And how have their places been filled? Truly, if evidence were ever wanting regarding the uncertainty of all that rests on earth, it might be found in a packet of old letters.

Source: *Chambers's Edinburgh Journal,* 1850.

5. The Little People of Our Great Towns

We live in an age and country which at least talk much of class grievances; and that everybody knows to be the first step, though perhaps a far-off one, to their removal! There is, however, an annually increasing class of Her Majesty's subjects whose peculiar disabilities have been championed by no pamphleteer, and represented by no petition to Parliament, nor has any honourable member yet pledged himself on hustings to attempt their remedy. It is not that the unfortunates themselves are voiceless; go to the streets and lanes of our cities – the poorer and more crowded the better – and you will hear them in summer afternoons, or in calm evenings when the spring is coming, send up their daily remonstrance. Ill worded, indeed it is, and unequal, now rising in shouts, now falling in broken murmurs, for the aggrieved subjects are children, who have known no daisied common, meadow-brook, or household garden; and the burden of the petition is – Room to play.

Reader, there is no treason against your gentility imagined; but if you live in a back street inhabited by honest artisans and small shopkeepers, near the busy heart of a great English town, your hearing the said petition cannot be a matter of choice, It will come in all forms, and at every season – through your window, open for air in the early summer, ring discordant shouts for the May, as a vendor of blossomed hawthorn passes. If your childhood has seen it whitening up old trees and hedgerows, think what theirs has missed. When you sit by the fire as the winter twilight falls calm and frosty, listen. They are singing old nursery rhymes hard by the old gin-palace. Look out on their poor plays – how circumscribed they are and meagre: trundling a hoop along the pavement, building banks in the gutter, and running small races from door to door. A real run or jump is not to be had; business has left no room for them. The streets belong to the grown-ups and their interests; and even these limited entertainments bring the rising generation in everybody's way. Ladies in pink bonnets put them aside with sour looks; the respectable householder who has lived there since the street was built, wonders their parents don't keep them within doors (he means in a two pair back); cab and omnibus threaten their very existence; and the policeman is to them a continual terror. There is probably a park within seven miles of their homes; their busy parents take them there some Sunday or holiday in their best clothes and behaviour, and they are afraid of damp grass or of walking too far.

Childhood in town and country are different things. O the green lanes where we wore out our shoes – the pools we fell into – the marshes in which we stuck fast, and feared nothing except our misadventures being found out at home! There were swings taken stealthily on old orchard-trees; there were garden-beds of our own, with London Pride or Sweet William in them – close by a southern wall where great cabbage-roses bloomed rich and red at midsummer. There were gatherings of everything that ripened in wood and dingle, from the first wild strawberry to the last of the haws.

The city-born can have no such memories. Their early world is one of brick and stone; its glory consists of shows and shop-windows; and its wisdom in the precocious knowledge of what can be had for a penny. Worse learning, doubtless, there is, even for children in large towns; but this is the common lot, not only of the working people's children, with whom our theme began, but of the heirs and successors of well-to-do respectability. Genteel street-children are not, indeed, scolded off the pavement, or chased out of the gutter; there is commonly a room in the house for them to play in, and a grassplot, with some acclimated trees, in most of the squares where they live. They see far more sights; they are taken oftener to the parks, and once a year to the country. But behold how early the compensation balance of life is made manifest; while the carpenter's five fir-twigs can rush down from the paternal mansion on the third floor, hoop in hand, to improve the shining minute, it requires two hours' hard dressing before a corresponding member of the mercantile or professional gentleman's olive-branches can go forth – hated, gloved, and maided – to take the morning air. Then, only think of the fine clothes that are to be taken care of under high penalties! How is Mary-Anne brought into bondage before her time to her laced polka; and the playtime of Master Tommy's existence sacrificed to his tunic! On the premature vanities thus instilled, let graver moralists discourse; a dressed-up child is a sad spectacle; and we never meet a group of little boys and girls, overlaid with their seniors' costly inventions, and kept in worship of the same by maid or mamma, without wishing, for their own sakes, that the silk were calico, and the velvet fustian.

Gathering Wild Flowers, taken from Pictures and Songs of Home (1861).

Could any benevolent fairy be found to accomplish that wish, many a young life might be happier, and many an old one wiser; but the fairies have left our world to trade and fashion; Cinderella's godmother and the queen of the lilies are gone even from country nurseries, for there also finery has come in with a flood; nevertheless, there are ditches and duck-ponds at hand; moreover, the proverb, out of sight out of mind, retains its ancient truth; and splendid hats and frocks run so many chances of injury, that they are apt to be reserved for occasions of ceremony.

Regarding city childhood, there is one question that has long puzzled us. Do its merely local memories haunt the pauses of after-life, like those that bind the dreams of country-born to hill and river? We know that hut or hall may become alike hallowed, because of the loving glance and tone whose like will meet us no more on this side of the skies – over these, time and place have no power; but does the gutter in the back-street, long pulled down and built over, return to the workman's visions, as the meadow-stream, with its primrose banks, comes back to those of the peasant's son? Can the second floor in the beer-shop over the way be remembered as vividly as the cottage among the corn? Will the grassplots and parks where the olive-branches went gloved etc, be dreamed of like the woody dells, where springs played up, and violets grew thick at the roots of old mossy trees? We cannot think they will; and if we are right, the players in park and gutter are spared one dreary experience – the vague and reasonless pining for the old place which comes over one in far-off times, when all he once knew are changed and gone, and there is nothing to be seen but graves and strangers.

After all, it may be that early scenes have their hold on the heart only through association. It is not the violet dingles, but life's violet days that we miss – not the home garden, but the fresh feelings with which we turned the mould. On that principle, what springs of pleasantness may well up from the memory of the back-street gutter – what summers may shine back through the recollection of the grassplots in the square!

There is then, something like real childhood in cities, in spite of pinched play, in spite of early business, yea, in spite of hats and tunics. Well, we wish it more room and better air, not forgetting its vested rights in butter-cups and daisies. Indeed, it has long been our private persuasion that families should be brought up only in the country. The idea occurs often, particularly at Guy Fawkes' time; and now a sound of promise rises through the march of civilisation. Science will win back to the workman's children their birthright that was sold for such a miserable mess. Has not everyone heard of the subterraneous railways intended to carry passengers from the utmost edge of London to its heart, for something between a half-penny and a farthing? Should that experiment succeed to the satisfaction of the shareholders – and there seems no cause of doubt – the close of our present century will probably see our cities surrounded by huge village-like suburbs, where households will live and children play, and fathers come home when work-shops close, leaving the crowded streets entirely to business, and citizens who own no other responsibility.

Readers, the time specified would not bring a raven to discretion; but they that interrupt your meditations with, 'Here we go round!' or 'All on a Monday morning!' will be gray before it comes. Be entreated then, for the luckless disturbers. If you must scold them from door or window – for human patience has limits – don't scold hard; and you, O gentle dames, who do the dressing of posterity, we know the awful necessities that require the little Whites to be as fine as the small Greens; but do make allowances for tumbles in the mud, admit the possibility of a scramble through dust and dead leaves, and more will be gained than ever was expected by this plea for the little people of our great towns!

Source: *Chambers's Edinburgh Journal,* 1854.

Appendix I

Frances Browne – The Main Events of her Life

1816	Born in Stranorlar, County Donegal.
1817	Blinded at the age of 18 months by smallpox.
1840	Her 1st poem to appear in print, in the *Londonderry Standard*.
1841	Her most famous poem, *Songs of our Land* was published in the *Irish Penny Journal*.
1844	Her 1st volume of poetry, *The Star of Atteghei, the Vision of Schwartz; and other Poems* was published.
1847	Moved to Edinburgh, accompanied by her sister Rebekah, who acted as her amanuensis. Her 2nd volume of poetry, *Lyrics and Miscellaneous Poems* was published.
1849-51	Her 12 'Legends of Ulster' appeared in *Tait's Edinburgh Magazine*.
1852	Moved to London, again accompanied by her sister.
1855	Her sister, Rebekah, married and moved to Scotland.
1856	Her 3rd volume of poetry, *Pictures and Songs of Home* was published. Her masterpiece, *Granny's Wonderful Chair, and its Tales of Fairy Times* was published.
1861	Her 1st novel, *My share of the World* was published.
1863	She was granted a Civil List Pension of £100 a year.
1866	She moved to Richmond-upon-Thames.
1867	She was declared bankrupt.
1869	*The Exile's Trust, and other Stories* was published.
1879	She died in Richmond on the 21st of August and was buried in the public cemetery there on the 25th of August.

Appendix II

A List of the Original Contributions Made by Frances Browne to Newspapers, Magazines and Periodicals.

Note: Although this list is fairly comprehensive, it is not a complete list as Frances wrote for so many magazines that it is very difficult, if not impossible, to identify them all. Note also that this list only contains original contributions and does not include the many places where her compositions were reprinted. The magazines etc. are listed, as far as possible, in chronological order, according to the year that she first made a contribution to their columns. It is also indicated whether she made just one, several (between 2 and 5) or many (more than 5) contributions to the publications listed.) And to conclude this survey, a list of the contributions that she made to *Chambers's Edinburgh Journal* for the year 1852 is shown in order to give readers some idea of the importance of this journal in her literary career.

The Londonderry Standard (one).
The Irish Penny Journal (several)
The Athenaeum (many)
The Nortern Whig (one)
The Keepsake (one)
The Mirror (several)
The Illuminated Magazine (several)
The Shilling Magazine (one)
Hood's Magazine (many)
Chamber's Edinburgh Journal (many)
Ainsworth's Magazine (one)
Fraser's Magazine (several)
The Rejected's Magazine (one)
The Truth Seeker (one)
The Family Herald (one)
The Belfast People's Magazine (several)
The Ulster Monthly Magazine (one)
The Dublin University Magazine (one)

The People's Journal (many)
The People's And Howitt's Journal (many)
Fulcher's Ladies Memorandum Book (many)
Hogg's Instructor (many)
The Torch (one)
Macphail's Edinburgh Ecclesiastical Journal (one)
The People's Press And Monthly Historical Newspaper (one)
Tait's Edinburgh Magazine (many)
The Domestic Journal (one)
The Scottish Agricultural Gazette (one)
Leigh Hunt's Journal (one)
The Lady's Newspaper (one)
The Ladies' Companion (many)
The British Journal (several)
The Critic (many)
The Dispatch (many)
The Leisure Hour (many)
The Morning Advertiser (one)
The Illustrated London News (one)
The Sunday At Home (many)
The Welcome Guest (several)

Articles Contributed to Chambers's Edinburgh Journal in the Year 1852.

The source of this information is the Chamber's archive in the National Library of Scotland and these articles were identified as coming from the pen of Frances Browne by Ms Ruth Boreham who was employed to carry out research there on my behalf. These were the stories and essays for which Browne was paid in the course of 1852 although it is possible that some of them may have appeared in the Journal either the year before or the year after. A rather similar list for almost any year between 1845 and 1870 could be supplied as Ms Boreham came across over a hundred contributions made during that quarter century.

Jan. 10th 1852 – Received from Messrs W & R Chambers the sum of six pounds five shillings being payment in full for writing No. 400

Losers, No.418 *Country Cousin* £2 and No. 421 *Wolf Gathering* £3 for publication in *Chambers's Edinburgh Journal*, and any other of their works in which they may hereafter wish to publish it.

Apr. 7th 1852 – Received from Messrs W & R Chambers the sum of two pounds ten shillings being payment in full for writing *The Legend of Amen Corner* for publication in *Chambers's Edinburgh Journal*, and in any other of their works.

Apr. 24th 1852 – Received from Messrs W & R Chambers the sum of three pounds being payment in full for writing *Tollman's Story* in No. 436 for publication in *Chambers's Edinburgh Journal* and any other of their works.

Aug 3rd 1852 – Received from Messrs W & R Chambers the sum of two pounds five shillings being payment in full for writing *Bill Williams* for publication in *Chambers's Edinburgh Journal* and any other of their works.

Sept. 18th 1852 – Received from Messrs W & R Chambers the sum of three pounds being payment in full for writing *The Tattleton Election* for publication in *Chambers's Edinburgh Journal* and any other of their works.

Nov. 30th 1852 – Received from Messrs W & R Chambers the sum of three pounds ten shillings being payment in full for writing *Giving the Basket* for publication in *Chambers's Edinburgh Journal* and any other of their works.

Appendix III – Further Reading

Anonymous, Biographical sketch of Frances Browne in Preface to ***The Star of Atteghei; the Vision of Schwartz; and other Poems*** (1844).

Anonymous, Biographical sketch of Frances Browne in ***Chambers's Journal*** (1861).

Gillian Avery, 'Frances Browne' in ***Oxford Dictionary of National Biography.***

Patrick Bonar, 'The Life and Works of Frances Browne' (2007).

Raymond Blair, 'Frances Browne and the Legends of Ulster' in ***Donegal Annual*** (2008).

Raymond Blair, 'Frances Browne' in ***Treasure Each Voice*** (2010), pages 737-744.

Raymond Blair, 'Blind Poetess Of Ulster: Photo Recently Discovered' in ***History Ireland*** May/June (2010).

George Crolly, 'The Life and Writings of Miss Brown, the blind poetess' in ***Dublin Review*** (December 1844).

Camilla Crosland, ***Landmarks of a Literary Life*** (1893) Pages 241-2.

Marya DeVoto, 'Frances Browne' in ***Dictionary Of Literary Biography*** (1999) Vol. 199.

Joseph Johnson, 'Frances Brown' in ***Clever Girls of Our Time*** (1862). Pages 174-188.

Linde Lunney, 'Frances Browne' in ***Dictionary Of Irish Biography*** (2010). See also online update of this Dictionary which contains amendments to the original article.

Paul Marchbanks 'Frances Browne' in ***Irish Women Writers: an A to Z Guide*** edited by A G Gonzalez (2006).

John McCall, 'Memoir of Frances Brown' in ***Young Ireland*** (1882).

Thomas McLean, 'Arms and the Circassian Woman' in **Victorian Poetry** (2003) Vol 41, No.3, pages 295-318.

Alice Mills, 'Happy endings in Hard Times and Granny's Wonderful Chair' in **The Victorian Fantasists** *(1991)* edited by Kath Filmer.

Dorothy Radford, preface to **Granny's Wonderful Chair,** 1908 edition.

Royal Literary Fund, Records on microfilm in the British Library.

Heather Tilley, 'Frances Browne: Toward a Poetics of Blind Writing' in **Journal of Literary and Cultural Disability Studies** (2009) Vol.3, issue 2.